序

"金银天然不是货币，但货币天然是金银。"

货币——这个人们熟悉而又陌生的宠儿，从历史的深处走来，它是商品经济内在矛盾的必然产物，也是深厚文化底蕴的层层积淀。从贝壳到毛皮，再到骨，最后到黄金等贵金属，一般等价物在不断变化演进，透过岁月的层层迷雾，你能聆听到历史的足响，感受到人类文明的不断进步。

可见，货币不只是流通手段，也不只是财富代表，它更是一种文化，因其反映了时代的技术和特征；它也是一种艺术，因其具有浓郁的民族特色和独特的艺术风格。

四千年的中国货币历史和货币文化，源远流长，博大精深，是华夏文明的重要组成部分。从原始社会末期出现贝币开始，以后不断涌现了各种形态的金属币。使用黄金铸造金币在我国可追溯到春秋战国时代。司马迁把金币称为上币，意指金币在各种由金属材料铸造成的钱币中地位最高。在我国源远流长的货币历史中，贵金属币占据了重要地位，在各个历史时期都可觅到它闪光的足迹——先秦时期楚国铸行的"郢爰"是我国现知最早的黄金铸币，先秦时期楚国铸行的"银空首布"是我国现知最早的白银铸币；汉代王莽钱中的"金错刀"、唐代的"金开元通宝"可称为贵金属纪念币的起源。

1979年国务院正式授权中国人民银行对外发行贵金属纪念币，1987年国务院批准成立了贵金属纪念币的唯一总经销单位——中国金币总公司。中国贵金属纪念币伴随着改革开放的春风应运而生，也从此走向了繁荣。三十年来，中国贵金属纪念币作为我国的法定货币——人民币的重要组成部分，已成为一颗璀璨的明珠闪耀在国际钱币界，为我国钱币文化增添了瑰丽的一笔。

2000年5月1日开始实施的《中华人民共和国人民币管理条例》明确界定，贵金属纪念币是具有特定主题的限量发行的人民币，其主题、面额、图案、材质、式样、规格、发行数量、发行时间等由中国人民银行确定，主题涉及重大政治、历史题材的，应当报国务院批准。

中国贵金属纪念币以弘扬中华钱币文化，展现中华文化风采和社会主义精神文明建设成就为宗旨，其诞生的时间虽晚，但成绩斐然，令人瞩目。1979年，为纪念中华人民共和国成立三十周年，中国人民银行发行了我国第一套贵金属纪念币。截至2014年底，中国现代贵金属纪念币已向海内外发行了10大系列、348个项目、2027个品种，中国已成为世界贵金属纪念币的主要出口国之一。这些纪念币题材丰富、设计新颖、铸造精良。置于手中，细细玩味，高品质，高品位。深厚文化，概括于方寸；无穷意蕴，浓缩于眼前。令人爱不释手，令人深味沉想。因而成为世界钱币之精品，受到广大钱币爱好者和收藏界的青睐。熊猫、生肖等题材的贵金属纪念币曾多次获得国内外大奖，熊猫普制金币成为国际钱币市场上享有盛誉的币种之一，也是国际五大投资币之一。

今天，随着物质与文化生活水平的不断提高，人们不再片面关注与张扬物质生活，不再以衣食、消费或金钱、权位来定义人生意义，不再被囚禁于物质与肉身生活的樊篱。人们不再像过去那样浮躁而庸俗，开始变得沉静而智慧，人们开始叩问自己的灵魂，开始敬重人性的高贵与神秘。总之，人们的收藏兴趣、观念以及投资方式都在发生着深刻的变化。贵金属纪念币以其独特的货币属性和蕴藏的文化属性而受到众多收藏者和投资者的青睐。特别是近几年来，随着我国现代贵金属纪念币发售体制的不断科学化，宣传力度的不断加大，越来越多的人开始关注贵金属纪念币，集藏和投资队伍日益扩大，贵金属纪念币已经成为收藏和投资领域的新宠。

为进一步弘扬中华钱币文化，推动中国金币事业的发展，提高收藏者和投资者对贵金属纪念币的鉴赏水平，中国金币总公司于2005年起陆续编纂出版《中华人民共和国贵金属纪念币图录》（以下简称《图录》）。《图录》出版以来，在业内引起强烈反响，受到业内专家、广大金银币集藏爱好者的欢迎和喜爱。自上次《图录》出版以来，中国金币事业继续蓬勃发展，奥运币成功发售，企业改制顺利推进，会员制营销体制改革初见成效，中国金币品牌不断深入人心，金币行业自律组织建设也在平稳推进。应社会各界的要求，按照编纂工作规划，我们将近五年发行的金银纪念币资料搜集整理，编纂出版了2010—2014年的《图录》精装本和2012—2014年的《图录》简装本。这两册书延续了《图录》的编纂风格，为广大钱币爱好者、收藏者和投资者提供了两本不可多得的参考工具书，读者会从中看到我国贵金属纪念币设计水平的不断提升和生产工艺的不断创新，体会到我国贵金属纪念币所蕴含的丰富的文化内涵，感受到中华民族灿烂的历史文明。该书具有以下特点：

1. 权威性。《图录》由中国金币总公司组织编纂。中国金币总公司成立于1987年，是我国唯一一家经营贵金属纪念币的专业公司。多年来，中国金币总公司汇集了一大批对贵金属纪念币发展演变历史相当熟悉，对贵金属纪念币的研究有着丰富实践经验和理论素养的专家学者。这样一支作者队伍，充分保证了《图录》的编纂质量。

2. 史料性。《图录》汇集了自1979年国务院授权中国人民银行发行贵金属币以来至2014年底发行的所有贵金属纪念币的正、背面图片和技术数据等重要资料，对中国贵金属纪念币三十五年来的发展历史进行了全面总结，完整、系统地反映出中国贵金属纪念币的发展脉络，是一部存史的力作，具有重要的史料价值。

3. 知识性。由于贵金属纪念币发行量小及价值高等因素的限制，社会上流传的贵金属纪念币实物并不多见，许多人可能几十年甚至终生都未曾见过。《图录》逼真地展示了贵金属纪念币的原貌，可方便人们了解人民币的这一重要币种，普及人民币知识。同时，中国贵金属纪念币题材丰富，囊括了国内外重大事件、中国及世界杰出人物、文体活动、珍稀动物、中国传统文化、中国古典文学名著、中国古代科技发明、中国名画、佛教艺术等方面的内容。丰富的币面主题，使《图录》具有了极强的知识性，充分反映出中华文明之博大精深、源远流长。

4. 艺术性。《图录》的艺术性体现在两个方面：《图录》所使用的贵金属纪念币图片，逼真地反映了币面设计的原貌，而贵金属纪念币的币面设计，本身具有很强的艺术性；《图录》一书设计精美，印装考究，作为一部画册，亦具有一定的鉴赏性。两方面的结合，使《图录》成为一件优秀的、非常具有鉴赏价值的艺术品。

5. 新颖性。《图录》注重了中国贵金属纪念币发展的时序性和系列性，做到发展轨迹清晰，系列脉络清晰，突出了内容编排和设计上的新颖性。

本册《图录》是集体劳动的果实，中国金币总公司和西南财经大学出版社的领导和许多同志都为这部图书的出版付出了辛勤的汗水，奉献了自己的才智。

作为一部大型工具书，尽管我们进行了大量的资料核实工作，但不足之处在所难免，我们诚恳希望各界朋友不吝赐教，以便我们今后改正。

中国金币总公司　2015年9月

Preface

Gold and silver are not naturally currency, but they are meant to be currency.

As the inevitable outcome of the immanent contradiction of commodity economy, currency—so familiar a concept for us all, enjoys a long history and brilliant culture. From shells to furs, animal bones, and eventually precious metals as gold, the universal equivalent evolves constantly. Through the ancient currency we can even hear the footsteps of history and feel the development of human civilization.

Therefore, currency is not merely means of circulation nor a simple represent for wealth but also a sort of culture. It reflects the technology and features of its time. Also, it is a sort of art, embracing strong national characteristics and unique artistic features.

Being a significant part of the splendid Huaxia culture, Chinese currency can trace its history back to ancient time and enjoy an extensive and profound culture. From the emergence of clam shells at the end of the primitive society, diverse metal currencies come forth later on. The use of minted gold as currency could be traced back to Spring and Autumn Period and Warring States Period. Sima Qian, a well-known Chinese historian, litterateur and ideologist in West Han dynasty, denominated gold currency as superior currency, implying the highest status of gold currency among other metal currencies. Precious metal currencies played an important role in ancient currency history which could be easily found in every historical period. "Ying Yuan" the earliest known gold minted coin emerged in Chu state in pre-Qin period, meaning love my state, so did silver "Kong Shou Bu" the earliest known silver coin, followed with gold "Cuo dao" in Han dynasty, meaning knife inlaid and gold "Kai Yuan Tong Bao" in Tang dynasty with the Chinese characters "kai yuan tong bao" on it. The latter two sorts of coins could be considered as the origin of commemorative precious metal coins.

In 1979, the People's Bank of China was authorized to issue commemorative precious metal coins by the State Council. The sole distribution institution of commemorative precious metal coins—China Gold Coin Incorporation was established in 1987 with the authorization by the State Council. From then on, commemorative precious metal coins become thriving in China, bathing in the spring breeze of the reform and opening up to the outside world. During the last three decades, Chinese commemorative precious metal coins, as legal tender, have become an essential part of Renminbi. They have also become a shining pearl in international numismatic field, drawing a marvelous picture in China's numismatic culture.

On May 1, 2000, *Regulation of the People's Republic of China on the Administration of Renminbi* came into effect, which declared that commemorative precious metal coins are legal tender of PRC with special themes and a limited mintage. The People's Bank of China shall determine their themes, designs, and specifications, such as metal content, finish quality, denomination, mintage and issuing date. However, themes of major political or historical importance shall be submitted to the State Council for approval.

Chinese commemorative precious metal coins are devoted to disseminating Chinese currency culture, spreading elegant Chinese culture and showing notable progress registered in socialist spiritual civilization construction. Late as Chinese commemorative precious metal coins emerged, remarkable achievements have been made. In 1979, the first set of commemorative precious metal coins were issued in commemoration of the 30th Anniversary of Founding of the People's Republic of China. Since then, 10 major coin categories with 348 coin programmes including 2027 items have been issued and China becomes one of the leading export countries of gold and silver commemorative coins. These coins are rich in themes, novel in designs, and exquisite in minting arts. Holding it in hand and lingering over its first-class quality and high grade, you can feel the brilliant and deep culture beyond the design as if the history appears again right in front of you. Their strong national features and unique artistic styles made many of them the cream in the world coin market, which are eagerly sought after by numismatists and coin collectors. Chinese gold and silver commemorative coins have won many awards in and out of China. Chinese Panda Gold Coin is one of the major investment coins in the international coin market.

With the continuous improvement of material and cultural living standard, people no longer pay attention to material life alone, nor just taking money and title as their ultimate goals. Instead, people now are pursuing calmness, wisdom and better spiritual life. They come to respect the dignity and mystery of humanity.

In a word, the enthusiasm and means of collecting are undergoing a great revolution. Because of the unique property of currency and profound culture features, commemorative precious metal coins attract more and more coin collectors and investors. In particular, more and more people become interested in commemorative precious metal currencies because of more scientific issuing system and better promotion. Collecting commemorative precious metal coins has been another good choice for collectors.

In order to further uphold Chinese numismatic culture, impel the development of Chinese gold coin industry and improve the appreciation level of collectors and investors, China Gold Coin Incorporation compiled from 2005 the Album of Precious Metal Commemorative Coins of the People's Republic of China.

Since the publication of *the Album*, it becomes very popular among coin experts and collectors and has received positive responses from the community. In the five years since its publication, have past since its publication, China gold coin industry continues its healthy and prosperous development: Beijing Olympic coin program has been successfully issued, the enterprise reform advances smoothly, marketing system reform on establishing membership sales has achieved initial success, China gold coin brand strikes deeper roots in the hearts of people, and gold coin self-discipline organization has been promoted favorably.

Upon the request of the society and our compilation plan, we collected all the materials from before and compiled hardcover edition of *the Album* (2010–2014) and paper cover edition of *the Album* (2012–2014). *The Albums* continue the compilation style of the previous ones and provide a valuable reference for coin collectors and investors. Through *the Albums*, readers can see the improvement and innovation of design level and production process and sense the rich culture and splendid Chinese history and civilization behind it.

The volumn has the following features:

1. Authority. *The Album* is compiled under the organization of China Gold Coin Incorporation which was established in 1987. As the only professional company under the direct leadership of the People's Bank of China dealing in gold and silver commemorative coins. Over the years, China Gold Coin Incorporation has always had close connections with many experts and scholars who are familiar with the history and evolvement of commemorative precious metal coins and have rich and practical experience and theory level in the study of commemorative precious metal currencies. Under their conductions and directions, *the Album* is certainly of high authority.

2. Historiography. *The Album* contains the obverse and reverse designs and important technical data of all coins issued by the People's Bank of China from 1979 till the end of 2014. It comprehensively concludes and systematically reflects the history and development of Chinese commemorative precious metal coins during the last 35 years. Therefore, *the Album* is of significant historic value.

3. Knowledge. Because of limited issuing quantity and high value, many people have little access to real commemorative precious metal coins. *The Album* vividly shows the practical appearance of commemorative precious metal coins which will contribute to popularizing knowledge about Renminbi and making people know more about this important legal tender. Besides, commemorative precious metal coins are rich in theme, reflecting information of domestic and international important events, Chinese and international worthies, recreational activities, rare animals, traditional Chinese culture, classical Chinese literature masterpieces, ancient Chinese technological inventions, traditional Chinese paintings and Buddhism, etc. Rich themes spread splendid Chinese history and brilliant culture while making *the Album* of great intellectual value.

4. Artistry. The artistry could be understood in two aspects: first, the pictures collected in *the Album* vividly show the practical appearance of the coins whose designs are of high artistic value; second, *the Album* itself is exquisitely designed and printed, which is worthy of appreciation and collection. Combining the two aspects together, it is no doubt that *the Album* is an art of great artistic value.

5. Novelty. Systematically arranged in chronological order, *the Album* clearly indicates the development of commemorative precious metal coins with clear systematic presentation. Great importance has been attached to novelty in design and layout.

The Album is the outcome of collective efforts. The leaders and professionals in China Gold Coin Incorporation and Southwest University of Finance and Economics Press make great contribution to producing *the Album*.

Although many research and collation have been done, as a reference book, it may be inevitable that some deficiencies exist. Yours remarks and suggestions are warmel welcomed.

China Gold Coin Incorporation
September 2015

凡例

中国人民银行从1979年开始发行现代贵金属纪念币，《中华人民共和国贵金属纪念币图录》收录了自1979—2014年的2000多个品种的贵金属纪念币。在中国贵金属纪念币发行早期，个别纪念币题材中包含有铜币，为反映中国贵金属纪念币的全貌，对这些铜币亦予收录。

一、本书以发行年代为序，按年编排；发行年与币面年号不一致的情况，按币面年号归年。各年发行的纪念币，除个别情况外，基本按发行时间顺序编排。

二、一套币分在多个年份发行的情况，如妈祖金银纪念币、马可·波罗金银纪念币等，集中在首发年反映，在其余年份的目录页作出标注，说明该年份发行的某某币已集中到哪一年。此外，对于已列入发行计划但实际未生产以及有样币而未发行的币种，在本书中均未收录。

三、每套纪念币所反映的内容包括：该套币的名称、每枚币的币面图案说明、编码、材质、质量、形制尺寸、重量、面额、成色、发行量、生产量、铸造单位、币面图案设计和模具雕刻作者。其中，“生产量”的反映只限于2000年及以后发行的纪念币，所反映的数据为总累积生产量；币面图案设计和模具雕刻作者分两种情况处理：2000年以前币品的作者作为附录在书末统一用大表列出，不一一对应币品；2000年以后币品下逐一标注作者姓名。

四、一套纪念币中，凡材质、外形及正面图案相同的情况，正面图案只出现一次，标明“共同正面”；材质、外形、规格、面额及正、背面图案相同，但重量不同的情况，即存在厚币和薄币的差别，其正、背面图案只反映厚币，在技术资料表格下，注明某某币为薄币。

五、在每套币的技术资料表格中，如果一套币全部为圆形，则“形制尺寸”一列以“直径”表示；若一套币为非圆形或多种形状混杂，则分别标注各枚币的形制尺寸。所有纪念币的正背面图片，均以与纪念币实物相同的大小进行反映。

六、为规范中国贵金属纪念币的发行和管理，方便读者阅读、鉴赏和检索，通过本书的出版，对每枚纪念币进行编码。编码标注在每枚币的背面图片下和技术资料表格中，图片下的编码与表格中的编码一一对应。编码规则如下：

（一）编码的构成

编码由五项基本要素组成，即币面年号、某年的第几套、套中的第几枚、材质、重量。按上述顺序排序，除某年的第几套和套中的第几枚两个要素连续反映外，各要素之间用“-”分隔。编码只针对正式发售的币品。

（二）关于熊猫币的编码

熊猫币作为贵金属币中的一个重要分支，肩负着投资币的功能，特在其编码中单独作出标识，熊猫币除五项基本要素之外，在编码最后标注符号“#”。

（三）各要素的表示方法

（1）编码中的“币面年号”要素使用4位数字的公元纪年。

（2）“某年第几套”和“套中的第几枚”分别采用2位阿拉伯数字，如某年的第一套即为01，其中的第一枚亦为01，第一套中的第一枚即为0101。“某年的第几套”按各套币的发售时间先后编排，下一年项目在上年底发行的，归入“币面年号”所在年的项目中，按实际发售顺序排列，其他以此类推。“套中的第几枚”，首先区分材质，不同材质的币，按金、银、铂、钯、双金属、铜的顺序编排；同一材质中，按重量由大到小编排；相同材质、相同重量的币，按精制、普制的顺序编排，同样质量的情况按主题反映的时间顺序排列，若主题时间顺序不明显则按惯例排序。

熊猫币的编码与上述原则略有不同，即：大部分年份的金币不是由大到小编排，而是将5个规格的普制金币排在最前面。

（3）“材质”用两个字母的化学元素符号表示，金、银、铂、钯、铜分别采用Au、Ag、Pt、Pd、Cu表示。双金属采用两种材质中间加“/”的形式标注。

（4）“重量”要素按照每枚币实际的重量来反映。盎司、公斤、克、两分别以oz、kg、g、tael标注。双金属采用据实反映重量的方式，标注各材质的重量，材质重量之间用“+”号分隔。

（5）本册中，所有“质量”是指贵金属纪念币的质量类型。

（6）本册中，浮雕制作者多处署名为“集体”，是指非个人以及创作小组一次性独立完成，或经过相互借鉴、多次修改等逐步完善创作。

七、为使技术资料表格尽量简洁，其中的“铸造单位”（国外厂家为代铸单位）一项未列出各厂家的全称，而采用了简化的形式。其简称、全称对应关系如下：

简称	全称
上海	上海造币有限公司（原上海造币厂）
沈阳	沈阳造币有限公司（原沈阳造币厂）
深圳	深圳国宝造币有限公司（原深圳国宝金币制造厂）
瑞士P	瑞士PAMP公司
瑞士F	瑞士FAUDE & HUGUENIN公司 （原瑞士HUGUENIN+KRAMER MEDAILLEURS公司）
瑞士V	瑞士VALCAMBI SA公司
澳大利亚	澳大利亚珀斯造币厂
加拿大	加拿大皇家造币厂

A Guide to the Use of the Album

Since the first issuance in 1979, The People's Bank of China has begun to issue commemorative precious metal coins. Altogether over 2000 coins issued from 1979 till 2014 are collected in the Album. In the beginning, some commemorative copper coins were minted. They are also included in this Album so as to draw an integral picture of commemorative precious metal coins.

I. This Album is arranged in chronological order with coins following one another according to their time of issuance. If the year of issuance is not in accordance with the year date, the year date counts.

II. One set of coins issued in several different years, as Mazu commemorative gold and silver coins and Marco Polo commemorative gold and silver coins, is put together in the light of the first year date of the sets, making notes in the contents of another year that this coin is converged in its sets. Such coins as being planned to issue but not produced or with only sample coins are not contained in this Album.

III. The information of each commemorative coin inclutes its name, explanation of its designs, code, metal, quality, dimension, weight, face value, fineness, mintage, actual mintage, minting authority, the designer and engraver. The "actual mintage" means the total quantity of each coin minted and this data makes sense only to the coins issued in and after the year 2000. Concerning the designers and engravers of the coins issued before the year 2000, their names are listed in capital in the appendix. The names of the designers and engravers of the coins issued after the year 2000 are put right below the coins.

IV. In any cases among a set, the metal, shape and obverse design of one coin are the same with another, the obverse design will just be shown once with notes "the common obverse design" for other coins. When only weight differs but with the same metal, shape, dimension, face value and designs, which means a thick coin and a thin coin of the same sort, only the obverse and reverse design of the thick coin is recorded, annotating in the technical data table the thin coin.

V. If all the coins in a set are round in shape, their diameters are denoted; if their shapes come all differently, each data is shown individually.

VI. In order to standardize the issue and management process, as well as to make it easier and more convenient for readers, a code is generated for each coin. The code is marked below the reverse design of the coin and in the technical data table. The coding formulae are as follows:

1. Factors of code.

Each code is made up of five factors: year date, the serial number of the set in the year, the serial number of the coin in the set, the serial mummer of its metal and its weight. All the five factors will be linked with "-" except the serial number of the set in the year and the serial number of the coin in the set. Only the coins issued and put on sale have such codes.

2. The code of the panda coin.

As an essential branch of precious metal coins, panda coin is also a kind of investment coin, whose code is different from other coins in the Album. At the end of each common code containing the five factors described above, a special mark of "#" is added to the panda coin.

3. The describing method of each code.

(1) Year date is expressed in four digits by the Christian era.

(2) The serial number of the set in the year and the serial number of the coin in the set are marked in two digits. For instance, the first set of a year is described as 01, the first coin of this set is marked 0101. The serial number follows one another by their time of issu-ance. The coins planned to issue the next year but are actually issued the end of the year earlier are marked according to their year time. The serial number of the coin in the set is classified firstly by the metal. The number follows the order of the metal as gold, silver, platinum, palladium, two-metal alloy and copper. Second, if the metal is the same and only weight differs, then from heavier to lighter. Third, when all the other factors are the same, follow the order of proof minted to bullion. Fourth, as for those with the same quality, the order is arranged according to the time order of the theme, and if there is not clear order of the theme then put in consistent with common practice.

However, the principles for panda coins are unlike those above. Most of the coins are not collocated by the size, but five gold bullion coins come first.

(3) Metal is described by chemical symbols. For example, gold, silver, platinum, palladium and copper are marked as Au, Ag, Pt, Pd and Cu respectively. Two-metal alloy is marked as two metals with a "/" in the middle.

(4) Factual weight of each coin is reflected and described by oz, kg, g and tael. When the coin is made by two-metal alloy, both of the weight are described linked by a "+".

(5) In the Album, Quality means whether the coin is proof minted or bullion.

(6) In the Album, if the relief sculptor writes collective, it means the relief is done by a group who have learnt from each other and made adjustments accordingly.

VII. To make the technical data table more concise, the name of the minting authority is abbreviated. The shortened form and its full name correspond as follows:

Shortened Form	Full Name
Shanghai	Shanghai Mint Co., Ltd.
Shenyang	Shenyang Mint Co., Ltd.
Shenzhen	Shenzhen Guobao Mint
Switzerland P	PAMP S. A.
Switzerland F	FAUDE & HUGUENIN
Switzerland V	VALCAMBI SA
Australia	The Perth Mint
Canada	Royal Canadian Mint

目录

Contents

2012

2010版熊猫金银纪念币
2010 Chinese Panda Gold and Silver Commemorative Coins

中国农业银行股份有限公司上市熊猫加字金银纪念币
Panda Commemorative Gold and Silver Coins for the Listing of Agricultural Bank of China Co., Ltd

中国资本市场20周年熊猫加字银质纪念币
Panda Commemorative Silver Coin for the 20th Anniversary of China's Capital Market

上海造币有限公司成立90周年熊猫加字金银纪念币
Panda Commemorative Gold and Silver Coins for the 90th Anniversary of Shanghai Mint

2010中国庚寅（虎）年金银纪念币
2010 Chinese Geng Yin Year (Year of the Tiger) Gold and Silver Commemorative Coins

中国古典文学名著——《水浒传》彩色金银纪念币（第2组）
The Chinese Famous Classical Literature Works – *Outlaws of the Marsh* Colored Gold and Silver Commemorative Coins (2nd Set)

中国2010年上海世界博览会金银纪念币（第2组）
The Official Commemorative Gold and Silver Coins for World EXPO 2010 Shanghai China (2nd Set)

第16届亚洲运动会金银纪念币（第2组）
The Official Commemorative Gold and Silver Coins of the 16th Asian Games (2nd Set)

世界遗产——武当山古建筑群金银纪念币
The Commemorative Gold and Silver Coins for World Heritage – Ancient Architectural Complex of Wudang Mountain

深圳经济特区建立30周年金银纪念币
The Commemorative Gold and Silver Coins for the 30th Anniversary of the Founding of Shenzhen Special Economic Zone

中国石窟艺术（云冈）金银纪念币
Chinese Grottoes Art (Yungang) Gold and Silver Commemorative Coins

中国京剧脸谱彩色金银纪念币（第1组）
Chinese Peking Opera Facial Mask Colored Commemorative Gold and Silver Coins (1st Set)

2010北京国际邮票钱币博览会银质纪念币
2010 Beijing International Stamp and Coin Exposition Commemorative Silver Coin

2010版熊猫金银纪念币

2010 Chinese Panda Gold and Silver Commemorative Coins

中国农业银行股份有限公司上市熊猫加字金银纪念币

Panda Commemorative Gold and Silver Coins for the Listing of Agricultural Bank of China Co., Ltd

中国资本市场20周年熊猫加字银质纪念币

Panda Commemorative Silver Coin for the 20th Anniversary of China's Capital Market

上海造币有限公司成立90周年熊猫加字金银纪念币

Panda Commemorative Gold and Silver Coins for the 90th Anniversary of Shanghai Mint

2010中国庚寅（虎）年金银纪念币

2010 Chinese Geng Yin Year (Year of the Tiger) Gold and Silver Commemorative Coins

中国古典文学名著——《水浒传》彩色金银纪念币（第2组）

The Chinese Famous Classical Literature Works – *Outlaws of the Marsh* Colored Gold and Silver Commemorative Coins (2nd Set)

中国2010年上海世界博览会金银纪念币（第2组）

The Official Commemorative Gold and Silver Coins for World EXPO 2010 Shanghai China (2nd Set)

第16届亚洲运动会金银纪念币（第2组）

The Official Commemorative Gold and Silver Coins of the 16th Asian Games (2nd Set)

世界遗产——武当山古建筑群金银纪念币

The Commemorative Gold and Silver Coins for World Heritage – Ancient Architectural Complex of Wudang Mountain

深圳经济特区建立30周年金银纪念币

The Commemorative Gold and Silver Coins for the 30th Anniversary of the Founding of Shenzhen Special Economic Zone

中国石窟艺术（云冈）金银纪念币

Chinese Grottoes Art (Yungang) Gold and Silver Commemorative Coins

中国京剧脸谱彩色金银纪念币（第1组）

Chinese Peking Opera Facial Mask Colored Commemorative Gold and Silver Coins (1st Set)

2010北京国际邮票钱币博览会银质纪念币

2010 Beijing International Stamp and Coin Exposition Commemorative Silver Coin

2010版熊猫金银纪念币

2010 Chinese Panda Gold and Silver Commemorative Coins

共同正面
正面图案：北京天坛祈年殿

编码：2010-0101-Au-1oz#
背面图案：熊猫双嬉图

编码：2010-0102-Au-1/2oz#
背面图案：熊猫双嬉图

编码：2010-0103-Au-1/4oz#
背面图案：熊猫双嬉图

编码：2010-0104-Au-1/10oz#
背面图案：熊猫双嬉图

编码：2010-0105-Au-1/20oz#
背面图案：熊猫双嬉图

本套币正面图稿设计者：孙奇龄
正面浮雕制作者：岳俊峰
背面图稿设计者：程　超
背面浮雕制作者：余　敏

金币7枚 银币3枚　7 Gold Coins 3 Silver Coins

编码	材质	质量	重量(盎司)	直径(毫米)	面额(元)	成色(%)	最大发行量(枚)	铸造单位
2010-0101-Au-1oz#	金币	普制	1	32	500	99.9	300000	深圳
2010-0102-Au-1/2oz#	金币	普制	1/2	27	200	99.9	120000	深圳
2010-0103-Au-1/4oz#	金币	普制	1/4	22	100	99.9	120000	深圳
2010-0104-Au-1/10oz#	金币	普制	1/10	18	50	99.9	120000	深圳
2010-0105-Au-1/20oz#	金币	普制	1/20	14	20	99.9	120000	深圳
2010-0106-Au-1kg#	金币	精制	1公斤	90	10000	99.9	200	沈阳
2010-0107-Au-5oz#	金币	精制	5	60	2000	99.9	1000	沈阳
2010-0108-Ag-1kg#	银币	精制	1公斤	100	300	99.9	4000	沈阳
2010-0109-Ag-5oz#	银币	精制	5	70	50	99.9	10000	沈阳
2010-0110-Ag-1oz#	银币	普制	1	40	10	99.9	1500000	上海、深圳

共同正面
正面图案：北京天坛祈年殿

编码：2010-0106-Au-1kg#
背面图案：熊猫双嬉图

编码：2010-0107-Au-5oz#
背面图案：熊猫双嬉图

共同正面
正面图案：北京天坛祈年殿

编码：2010-0108-Ag-1kg#
背面图案：熊猫双嬉图

2010版熊猫金银纪念币

2010 Chinese Panda Gold and Silver Commemorative Coins

编码：2010-0109-Ag-5oz#
背面图案：熊猫双嬉图

正面图案：北京天坛祈年殿

编码：2010-0110-Ag-1oz#
背面图案：熊猫双嬉图

中国农业银行股份有限公司上市熊猫加字金银纪念币

Panda Commemorative Gold and Silver Coins for the Listing of Agricultural Bank of China Co., Ltd

正面图案：北京天坛祈年殿

编码：2010-0701-Au-1/4oz#
背面图案：熊猫双嬉图

正面图案：北京天坛祈年殿

编码：2010-0702-Ag-1oz#
背面图案：熊猫双嬉图

本套币正面图稿设计者：孙奇龄
正面浮雕制作者：岳俊峰
背面图稿设计者：程　超
背面浮雕制作者：余　敏

金币1枚　银币1枚　1 Gold Coin　1 Silver Coin

编码	材质	质量	重量(盎司)	直径(毫米)	面额(元)	成色(%)	最大发行量(枚)	铸造单位
2010-0701-Au-1/4oz#	金币	普制	1/4	22	100	99.9	60000	深圳
2010-0702-Ag-1oz#	银币	普制	1	40	10	99.9	70000	深圳

中国资本市场20周年熊猫加字银质纪念币

Panda Commemorative Silver Coin for the 20th Anniversary of China's Capital Market

正面图案：北京天坛祈年殿

编码：2010-1201-Ag-1oz#

背面图案：熊猫双嬉图

本套币正面图稿设计者：孙奇龄
正面浮雕制作者：岳俊峰
背面图稿设计者：程 超
背面浮雕制作者：余 敏

银币1枚 1 Silver Coin

编码	材质	质量	重量(盎司)	直径(毫米)	面额(元)	成色(%)	最大发行量(枚)	铸造单位
2010-1201-Ag-1oz#	银币	普制	1	40	10	99.9	40000	深圳

上海造币有限公司成立90周年熊猫加字金银纪念币

Panda Commemorative Gold and Silver Coins for the 90th Anniversary of Shanghai Mint

正面图案：北京天坛祈年殿

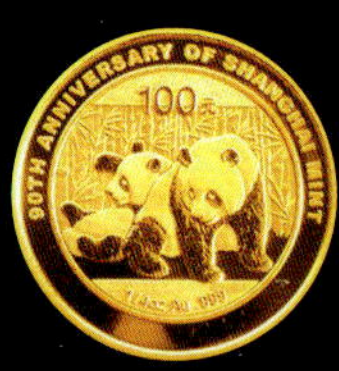

编码：2010-1301-Au-1/4oz#
背面图案：熊猫双嬉图

正面图案：北京天坛祈年殿

编码：2010-1302-Ag-1oz#
背面图案：熊猫双嬉图

本套币正面图稿设计者：孙奇龄
正面浮雕制作者：岳俊峰
背面图稿设计者：程　超
背面浮雕制作者：余　敏

金币1枚　银币1枚　1 Gold Coin　1 Silver Coin

编码	材质	质量	重量(盎司)	直径(毫米)	面额(元)	成色(%)	最大发行量(枚)	铸造单位
2010-1301-Au-1/4oz#	金币	普制	1/4	22	100	99.9	5000	上海
2010-1302-Ag-1oz#	银币	普制	1	40	10	99.9	20000	上海

上海造币有限公司成立90周年熊猫加字金银纪念币

Panda Commemorative Gold and Silver Coins for the 90th Anniversary of Shanghai Mint

2010中国庚寅（虎）年金银纪念币

2010 Chinese Geng Yin Year (Year of the Tiger) Gold and Silver Commemorative Coins

正面图案：中华人民共和国国徽及连年有余吉祥纹饰
设计者：张文静
浮雕制作者：集体

2010中国庚寅（虎）年金银纪念币

2010 Chinese Geng Yin Year (Year of the Tiger) Gold and Silver Commemorative Coins

编码：2010-0201-Au-10kg
背面图案：卧虎图及装饰虎头
设计者：朱熙华　何云
浮雕制作者：宋飞

正面图案：
中华人民共和国国徽及连年有余吉祥纹饰
设计者：张文静
浮雕制作者：集体

2010中国庚寅（虎）年金银纪念币

2010 Chinese Geng Yin Year (Year of the Tiger) Gold and Silver Commemorative Coins

编码：2010-0202-Au-1kg
背面图案：卧虎图及装饰虎头
设计者：朱熙华　何云
浮雕制作者：宋飞

正面图案：
中华人民共和国国徽及连年有余吉祥纹饰
设计者：张文静
浮雕制作者：集体

编码：2010-0203-Au-5oz
背面图案：中国民间传统装饰虎图形及吉祥花卉
设计者：张文静　何忠
浮雕制作者：邓姗姗

金币8枚　银币7枚　8 Gold Coins　7 Silver Coins

编码	材质	质量	重量(盎司)	形制尺寸(毫米)	面额(元)	成色(%)	最大发行量(枚)	铸造单位
2010-0201-Au-10kg	金币	精制	10公斤	圆形直径180	100000	99.9	18	深圳
2010-0202-Au-1kg	金币	精制	1公斤	梅花形外接圆直径100	10000	99.9	118	深圳
2010-0203-Au-5oz	彩色金币	精制	5	圆形直径60	2000	99.9	1800	深圳
2010-0204-Au-5oz	金币	精制	5	长方形60×40	2000	99.9	118	深圳
2010-0205-Au-1/2oz	金币	精制	1/2	梅花形外接圆直径27	200	99.9	8000	深圳
2010-0206-Au-1/2oz	金币	普制	1/2	扇形外圆半径58,内圆半径39,圆心角30度	200	99.9	6600	深圳
2010-0207-Au-1/10oz	彩色金币	精制	1/10	圆形直径18	50	99.9	80000	上海
2010-0208-Au-1/10oz	金币	精制	1/10	圆形直径18	50	99.9	80000	深圳
2010-0209-Ag-1kg	银币	精制	1公斤	圆形直径100	300	99.9	3800	深圳
2010-0210-Ag-5oz	彩色银币	精制	5	圆形直径70	50	99.9	8800	深圳
2010-0211-Ag-5oz	银币	精制	5	长方形80×50	50	99.9	1888	深圳
2010-0212-Ag-1oz	彩色银币	精制	1	圆形直径40	10	99.9	100000	沈阳
2010-0213-Ag-1oz	银币	精制	1	梅花形外接圆直径40	10	99.9	60000	深圳
2010-0214-Ag-1oz	银币	普制	1	扇形外接圆半径85,内圆半径60,圆心角30度	10	99.9	66000	深圳
2010-0215-Ag-1oz	银币	精制	1	圆形直径40	10	99.9	100000	深圳

正面图案：中华人民共和国国徽及连年有余吉祥纹饰
设计者：张文静
浮雕制作者：集体

编码：2010-0204-Au-5oz
背面图案：卧虎图及装饰虎头
设计者：朱熙华　何云
浮雕制作者：宋飞

正面图案：甘肃酒泉鼓楼
设计者：曾成沪
浮雕制作者：钟承辛

编码：2010-0206-Au-1/2oz
背面图案：卧虎图及装饰虎头
设计者：朱熙华　何云
浮雕制作者：宋飞

正面图案：中华人民共和国国徽及连年有余吉祥纹饰
设计者：张文静
浮雕制作者：集体

编码：2010-0205-Au-1/2oz
背面图案：卧虎图及装饰虎头
设计者：朱熙华　何云
浮雕制作者：宋飞

2010中国庚寅（虎）年金银纪念币

2010 Chinese Geng Yin Year (Year of the Tiger) Gold and Silver Commemorative Coins

共同正面
正面图案：中华人民共和国国徽及连年有余吉祥纹饰
设计者：张文静
浮雕制作者：集体

编码：2010-0207-Au-1/10oz
背面图案：中国民间传统装饰虎图形及吉祥花卉
设计者：张文静　何忠
浮雕制作者：张春晔

编码：2010-0208-Au-1/10oz
背面图案：卧虎图及装饰虎头
设计者：朱熙华　何云
浮雕制作者：宋飞

正面图案：中华人民共和国国徽
及连年有余吉祥纹饰
设计者：张文静　浮雕制作者：集体

编码：2010-0209-Ag-1kg
背面图案：卧虎图及装饰虎头
设计者：朱熙华　何云　浮雕制作者：宋飞

正面图案：中华人民共和国国徽
及连年有余吉祥纹饰
设计者：张文静
浮雕制作者：集体

编码：2010-0210-Ag-5oz
背面图案：中国民间传统装饰虎图形
及吉祥花卉
设计者：张文静　何忠
浮雕制作者：邓姗姗

正面图案：中华人民共和国国徽
及连年有余吉祥纹饰
设计者：张文静
浮雕制作者：集体

2010中国庚寅（虎）年金银纪念币

2010 Chinese Geng Yin Year (Year of the Tiger) Gold and Silver Commemorative Coins

编码：2010-0211-Ag-5oz
背面图案：卧虎图及装饰虎头
设计者：朱熙华　何云
浮雕制作者：宋飞

正面图案：
中华人民共和国国徽及连年有余吉祥纹饰
设计者：张文静
浮雕制作者：集体

编码：2010-0212-Ag-1oz
背面图案：中国民间传统装饰虎图形及吉祥花卉
设计者：张文静　何忠
浮雕制作者：邓姗姗

正面图案：
中华人民共和国国徽及连年有余吉祥纹饰
设计者：张文静
浮雕制作者：集体

编码：2010-0213-Ag-1oz
背面图案：卧虎图及装饰虎头
设计者：朱熙华　何云
浮雕制作者：宋飞

正面图案：甘肃酒泉鼓楼
设计者：曾成沪
浮雕制作者：钟承辛

编码：2010-0214-Ag-1oz
背面图案：卧虎图及装饰虎头
设计者：朱熙华　何云
浮雕制作者：宋飞

正面图案：
中华人民共和国国徽及连年有余吉祥纹饰
设计者：张文静
浮雕制作者：集体

编码：2010-0215-Ag-1oz
背面图案：卧虎图及装饰虎头
设计者：朱熙华　何云
浮雕制作者：宋飞

2010中国庚寅（虎）年金银纪念币

2010 Chinese Geng Yin Year (Year of the Tiger) Gold and Silver Commemorative Coins

正面图案：中华人民共和国国徽及中国传统纹样
设计者：李继业
浮雕制作者：马光华

中国古典文学名著——《水浒传》彩色金银纪念币（第2组）

The Chinese Famous Classical Literature Works—*Outlaws of the Marsh*
Colored Gold and Silver Commemorative Coins (2nd Set)

编码：2010-0301-Au-5oz
背面图案：三打祝家庄
设计者：张磊　浮雕制作者：董慧珍

金币2枚　银币3枚　2 Gold Coins　3 Silver Coins

编码	材质	质量	重量(盎司)	形制尺寸(毫米)	面额(元)	成色(%)	最大发行量(枚)	铸造单位
2010-0301-Au-5oz	彩色金币	精制	5	长方形64×40	2000	99.9	900	上海
2010-0302-Au-1/3oz	彩色金币	精制	1/3	圆形直径23	150	99.9	35000	深圳
2010-0303-Ag-5oz	彩色银币	精制	5	长方形80×50	50	99.9	12000	深圳
2010-0304-Ag-1oz	彩色银币	精制	1	圆形直径40	10	99.9	70000	上海
2010-0305-Ag-1oz	彩色银币	精制	1	圆形直径40	10	99.9	70000	深圳

正面图案：中华人民共和国国徽及中国传统纹样
设计者：李继业
浮雕制作者：曾成沪

编码：2010-0302-Au-1/3oz
背面图案：卢俊义
设计者：张磊
浮雕制作者：魏雪飞

正面图案：中华人民共和国国徽及中国传统纹样
设计者：李继业
浮雕制作者：马光华

编码：2010-0303-Ag-5oz
背面图案：公孙胜斗法破高廉
设计者：张磊
浮雕制作者：禹飞

正面图案：中华人民共和国国徽及中国传统纹样
设计者：李继业
浮雕制作者：马光华

编码：2010-0304-Ag-1oz
背面图案：杨志卖刀
设计者：张磊　浮雕制作者：黄喆

正面图案：中华人民共和国国徽及中国传统纹样
设计者：李继业　浮雕制作者：马光华

中国古典文学名著——《水浒传》彩色金银纪念币（第2组）

The Chinese Famous Classical Literature Works—*Outlaws of the Marsh*
Colored Gold and Silver Commemorative Coins (2nd Set)

编码：2010-0305-Ag-1oz
背面图案：武松打虎
设计者：张磊　浮雕制作者：宋飞

中国2010年上海世界博览会金银纪念币（第2组）

The Official Commemorative Gold and Silver Coins for World EXPO 2010 Shanghai China (2nd Set)

编码：2010-0402-Au-1/3oz
背面图案：中国馆建筑造型
设计者：王虎鸣
浮雕制作者：钟承辛

共同正面
正面图案：中国2010年上海世界博览会会徽、地球图案
设计者：赵樯
浮雕制作者：禹飞

编码：2010-0401-Au-5oz
背面图案：中国馆建筑造型
设计者：王虎鸣
浮雕制作者：钟承辛

共同正面
正面图案：中国2010年上海世界博览会会徽、地球图案
设计者：赵樯
浮雕制作者：袁晨　常智　刘鸿鹏

编码：2010-0403-Ag-1oz
背面图案：人物剪影、盛开的鲜花与寓意科技发展元素的装饰图案
设计者：全剑峰　鲁丹叶
浮雕制作者：常欢　富丽莉

编码：2010-0404-Ag-1oz
背面图案：飞翔的鸽子、盛开的鲜花与寓意宇宙太空元素的装饰图案
设计者：全剑峰　鲁丹叶
浮雕制作者：王文栋

金币2枚　银币2枚　2 Gold Coins　2 Silver Coins

编码	材质	质量	重量(盎司)	直径(毫米)	面额(元)	成色(%)	最大发行量(枚)	铸造单位
2010-0401-Au-5oz	金币	精制	5	60	2000	99.9	1000	深圳
2010-0402-Au-1/3oz	金币	精制	1/3	23	150	99.9	60000	深圳
2010-0403-Ag-1oz	银币	精制	1	40	10	99.9	80000	沈阳
2010-0404-Ag-1oz	银币	精制	1	40	10	99.9	80000	上海

第16届亚洲运动会金银纪念币（第2组）

The Official Commemorative Gold and Silver Coins of the 16th Asian Games (2nd Set)

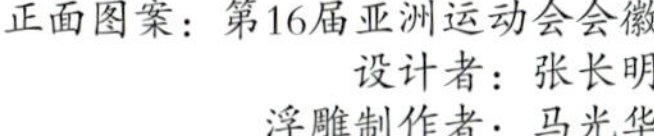

正面图案：第16届亚洲运动会会徽
设计者：张长明
浮雕制作者：马光华

编码：2010-0501-Au-1/4oz
背面图案：广州亚运城
综合体育馆、焰火
设计者：周剑
浮雕制作者：钟承辛

正面图案：第16届亚洲运动会会徽
设计者：张长明
浮雕制作者：马光华

编码：2010-0502-Ag-1oz
背面图案：排球、足球、体操运动员造型
设计者：朱熙华
浮雕制作者：宋飞

全币1枚 银币1枚 1 Gold Coin 1 Silver Coin

编码	材质	质量	重量(盎司)	直泾(毫米)	面额(元)	成色(%)	最大发行量(枚)	铸造单位
2010-0501-Au-1/4oz	金币	精制	1/4	22	100	99.9	30000	深圳
2010-0502-Ag-1oz	银币	精制	1	40	10	99.9	60000	深圳

聖廷苑酒店
SEG TECHNOLOGY PARK

深圳经济特区建立30周年金银纪念币

The Commemorative Gold and Silver Coins for the 30th Anniversary of the Founding of Shenzhen Special Economic Zone

正面图案：中华人民共和国国徽及簕杜鹃花纹样
设计者：姚有均
浮雕制作者：禹飞

编码：2010-0801-Au-1/4oz
背面图案：“拓荒牛”雕塑剪影及建筑、光束、礼花
设计者：广州东方红文化策划传播有限公司
浮雕制作者：钟承辛

正面图案：中华人民共和国国徽及簕杜鹃花纹样
设计者：姚有均
浮雕制作者：禹飞

编码：2010-0802-Ag-1oz
背面图案：人物头部剪影与抽象符号及“闯”雕塑
设计者：蔡寅昱
浮雕制作者：邓姗姗

金币1枚 银币1枚 1 Gold Coin 1 Silver Coin

编码	材质	质量	重量(盎司)	直径(毫米)	面额(元)	成色(%)	最大发行量(枚)	铸造单位
2010-0801-Au-1/4oz	金币	精制	1/4	22	100	99.9	20000	深圳
2010-0802-Ag-1oz	银币	精制	1	40	10	99.9	30000	深圳

中国石窟艺术（云冈）金银纪念币

Chinese Grottoes Art (Yungang) Gold and Silver Commemorative Coins

正面图案：云冈石窟外景
设计者：富丽莉
浮雕制作者：宋飞

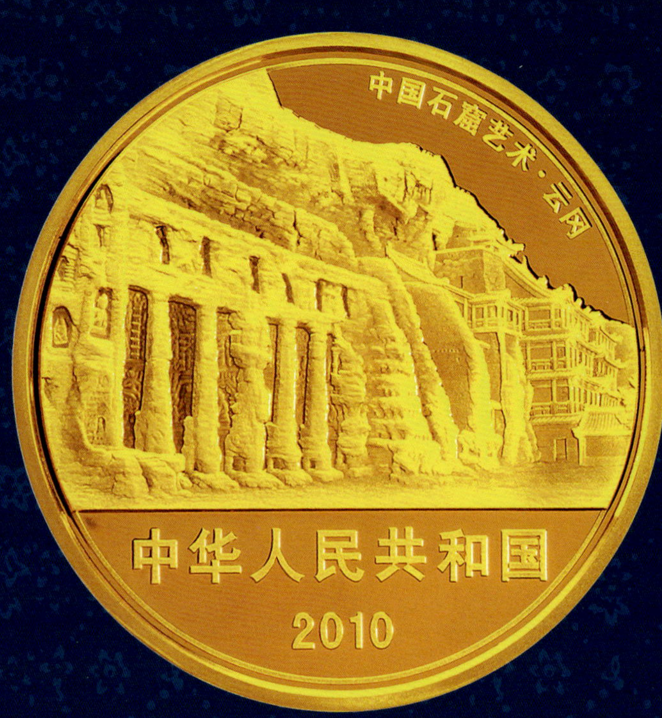

编码：2010-0901-Au-1kg
背面图案：三世佛像
设计者：周剑
浮雕制作者：张江

金币3枚 银币2枚 3 Gold Coins 2 Silver Coins

编码	材质	质量	重量(盎司)	直径(毫米)	面额(元)	成色(%)	最大发行量(枚)	铸造单位
2010-0901-Au-1kg	金币	精制	1公斤	90	10000	99.9	100	深圳
2010-0902-Au-5oz	金币	精制	5	60	2000	99.9	800	深圳
2010-0903-Au-1/2oz	金币	精制	1/2	27	200	99.9	10000	深圳
2010-0904-Ag-1kg	银币	精制	1公斤	100	300	99.9	3800	沈阳
2010-0905-Ag-2oz	银币	精制	2	40	20	99.9	20000	深圳

正面图案：云冈石窟外景
设计者：富丽莉
浮雕制作者：宋飞

编码：2010-0902-Au-5oz
背面图案：太子乘象回城图
设计者：白牧
浮雕制作者：常欢　富丽莉

中国石窟艺术（云冈）金银纪念币

Chinese Grottoes Art (Yungang) Gold and Silver Commemorative Coins

正面图案：云冈石窟外景
设计者：富丽莉
浮雕制作者：宋飞

编码：2010-0903-Au-1/2oz
背面图案：坐佛头像
设计者：王玲
浮雕制作者：宋飞

正面图案：云冈石窟外景
设计者：富丽莉
浮雕制作者：宋飞

编码：2010-0904-Ag-1kg
背面图案：菩萨像与莲花纹
设计者：余敏
浮雕制作者：廖博

正面图案：云冈石窟外景
设计者：富丽莉
浮雕制作者：宋飞

编码：2010-0905-Ag-2oz
背面图案：莲花与飞天图
设计者：张长明
浮雕制作者：魏雪飞

中国京剧脸谱彩色金银纪念币（第1组）

Chinese Peking Opera Facial Mask Colored Commemorative Gold and Silver Coins (1st Set)

正面图案：中华人民共和国国徽及海水江牙、祥云
设计者：王虎鸣
浮雕制作者：黄喆 胥瑜婷

编码：2010-1001-Au-1/4oz
背面图案："包拯"京剧脸谱
设计者：王虎鸣
浮雕制作者：刘鸿鹏 富丽莉 王刚

正面图案：中华人民共和国国徽及海水江牙、祥云
设计者：王虎鸣
浮雕制作者：黄喆 胥瑜婷

编码：2010-1002-Ag-1oz
背面图案："钟馗"京剧脸谱
设计者：王虎鸣
浮雕制作者：刘鸿鹏 富丽莉 王刚

正面图案：中华人民共和国国徽及海水江牙、祥云
设计者：王虎鸣
浮雕制作者：黄喆 胥瑜婷

编码：2010-1003-Ag-1oz
背面图案："典韦"京剧脸谱
设计者：王虎鸣
浮雕制作者：刘鸿鹏 富丽莉 王刚

金币1枚 银币2枚 1 Gold Coin 2 Silver Coins

编码	材质	质量	重量(盎司)	直径(毫米)	面额(元)	成色(%)	最大发行量(枚)	铸造单位
2010-1001-Au-1/4oz	彩色金币	精制	1/4	22	100	99.9	30000	上海
2010-1002-Ag-1oz	彩色银币	精制	1	40	10	99.9	50000	沈阳
2010-1003-Ag-1oz	彩色银币	精制	1	40	10	99.9	50000	沈阳

2010北京国际邮票钱币博览会银质纪念币

2010 Beijing International Stamp and Coin Exposition Commemorative Silver Coin

正面图案：象征钱币的圆点和装饰线与2010北京国际邮票钱币博览会会标

设计者：朱熙华　浮雕制作者：马光华

编码：2010-1101-Ag-1oz

背面图案：中国唐代方孔圆钱与阿拉伯阿巴斯王朝钱币

设计者：齐云兰　浮雕制作者：谢欣锐

银币1枚　1 Silver Coin

编码	材质	质量	重量(盎司)	直径(毫米)	面额(元)	成色(%)	最大发行量(枚)	铸造单位
2010-1101-Ag-1oz	银币	精制	1	40	10	99.9	30000	上海

2010北京国际邮票钱币博览会银质纪念币

2010 Beijing International Stamp and Coin Exposition Commemorative Silver Coin

2011

2011版熊猫金银纪念币

2011 Chinese Panda Gold and Silver Commemorative Coins

新中国航空工业建立60周年熊猫加字金银纪念币

Panda Commemorative Gold and Silver Coins for the 60th Anniversary of Aviation Industry of P. R. China

2011西安世界园艺博览会熊猫加字金银纪念币

Panda Commemorative Gold and Silver Coins for the International Horticultural Exposition 2011 Xi'an China

京沪高速铁路开通熊猫加字金银纪念币

Panda Commemorative Gold and Silver Coins for Beijing – Shanghai High Speed Rail Opening to Traffic

中国金融工会全国委员会成立60周年熊猫加字纪念银币

The Panda Commemorative Silver Coins for the 60th Anniversary of the National Committee of the Chinese Financial Workers' Union

上海黄金交易所成立10周年熊猫加字金银纪念币

Panda Commemorative Gold and Silver Coins for the 10th Anniversary of Shanghai Gold Exchange

厦门经济特区建设30周年熊猫加字金银纪念币

Panda Commemorative Gold and Silver Coins for the 30th Anniversary of Xiamen Special Economic Zone

新中国农村信用社成立60周年熊猫加字金银纪念币

Panda Commemorative Gold and Silver Coins for the 60th Anniversary

of the Rural Credit Cooperatives of P.R. China

2011中国辛卯（兔）年金银纪念币

2011 Chinese Xin Mao Year (Year of the Rabbit) Gold and Silver Commemorative Coins

中国京剧脸谱彩色金银纪念币（第2组）

Chinese Peking Opera Facial Mask Colored Commemorative Gold and Silver Coins (2nd Set)

深圳第26届世界大学生夏季运动会金银纪念币

The Commemorative Gold and Silver Coins for the 26th Summer Universiade, Shenzhen

世界自然基金会成立50周年金银纪念币

The Official Commemorative Gold and Silver Coins for the 50th Anniversary of the World Wide Fund for Nature (WWF)

清华大学建校100周年金银纪念币

The Official Commemorative Gold and Silver Coins for Tsinghua University Centenary Celebration

世界遗产——登封“天地之中”历史建筑群金银纪念币

The Official Commemorative Gold and Silver Coins of the Historical Monuments of Dengfeng in "the Centre of Heaven and Earth"

西藏和平解放60周年金银纪念币

The Commemorative Gold and Silver Coins for the 60th Anniversary of the Peaceful Liberation of Tibet

辛亥革命100周年金银纪念币

The Commemorative Gold and Silver Coins for the 100th Anniversary of Xinhai Revolution

2011北京国际钱币博览会银质纪念币

2011 Beijing International Coin Exposition Commemorative Silver Coins

中国古典文学名著——《水浒传》彩色金银纪念币（第3组）

The Chinese Famous Classical Literature Works – *Outlaws of the Marsh* Colored Gold and Silver Commemorative Coins (3rd Set)

2011版熊猫金银纪念币

2011 Chinese Panda Gold and Silver Commemorative Coins

新中国航空工业建立60周年熊猫加字金银纪念币

Panda Commemorative Gold and Silver Coins for the 60th Anniversary of Aviation Industry of P. R. China

2011西安世界园艺博览会熊猫加字金银纪念币

Panda Commemorative Gold and Silver Coins for the International Horticultural Exposition 2011 Xi'an China

京沪高速铁路开通熊猫加字金银纪念币

Panda Commemorative Gold and Silver Coins for Beijing – Shanghai High Speed Rail Opening to Traffic

中国金融工会全国委员会成立60周年熊猫加字纪念银币

The Panda Commemorative Silver Coins for the 60th Anniversary of the National Committee of the Chinese Financial Workers' Union

上海黄金交易所成立10周年熊猫加字金银纪念币

Panda Commemorative Gold and Silver Coins for the 10th Anniversary of Shanghai Gold Exchange

厦门经济特区建设30周年熊猫加字金银纪念币

Panda Commemorative Gold and Silver Coins for the 30th Anniversary of Xiamen Special Economic Zone

新中国农村信用社成立60周年熊猫加字金银纪念币

Panda Commemorative Gold and Silver Coins for the 60th Anniversary of the Rural Credit Cooperatives of P.R. China

2011中国辛卯（兔）年金银纪念币

2011 Chinese Xin Mao Year (Year of the Rabbit) Gold and Silver Commemorative Coins

中国京剧脸谱彩色金银纪念币（第2组）

Chinese Peking Opera Facial Mask Colored Commemorative Gold and Silver Coins (2nd Set)

深圳第26届世界大学生夏季运动会金银纪念币

The Commemorative Gold and Silver Coins for the 26th Summer Universiade, Shenzhen

世界自然基金会成立50周年金银纪念币

The Official Commemorative Gold and Silver Coins for the 50th Anniversary of the World Wide Fund for Nature (WWF)

清华大学建校100周年金银纪念币

The Official Commemorative Gold and Silver Coins for Tsinghua University Centenary Celebration

世界遗产——登封“天地之中”历史建筑群金银纪念币

The Official Commemorative Gold and Silver Coins of the Historical Monuments of Dengfeng in "the Centre of Heaven and Earth"

西藏和平解放60周年金银纪念币

The Commemorative Gold and Silver Coins for the 60th Anniversary of the Peaceful Liberation of Tibet

辛亥革命100周年金银纪念币

The Commemorative Gold and Silver Coins for the 100th Anniversary of Xinhai Revolution

2011北京国际钱币博览会银质纪念币

2011 Beijing International Coin Exposition Commemorative Silver Coins

中国古典文学名著——《水浒传》彩色金银纪念币（第3组）

The Chinese Famous Classical Literature Works – Outlaws of the Marsh Colored Gold and Silver Commemorative Coins (3rd Set)

2011版熊猫金银纪念币

2011 Chinese Panda Gold and Silver Commemorative Coins

共同正面
正面图案：北京天坛祈年殿

编码：2011-0201-Au-1oz#
背面图案：母子熊猫图

编码：2011-0202-Au-1/2oz#
背面图案：母子熊猫图

编码：2011-0203-Au-1/4oz#
背面图案：母子熊猫图

编码：2011-0204-Au-1/10oz#
背面图案：母子熊猫图

编码：2011-0205-Au-1/20oz#
背面图案：母子熊猫图

本套币正面图稿设计者：孙奇龄
正面浮雕制作者：岳俊峰
背面图稿设计者：赵　樯
背面浮雕制作者：宋　飞

金币7枚　银币3枚　7 Gold Coins 3 Silver Coins

编码	材质	质量	重量(盎司)	直径(毫米)	面额(元)	成色(%)	最大发行量(枚)	铸造单位
2011-0201-Au-1oz#	金币	普制	1	32	500	99.9	500000	深圳、上海
2011-0202-Au-1/2oz#	金币	普制	1/2	27	200	99.9	600000	深圳、上海
2011-0203-Au-1/4oz#	金币	普制	1/4	22	100	99.9	600000	深圳、上海
2011-0204-Au-1/10oz#	金币	普制	1/10	18	50	99.9	600000	深圳、上海
2011-0205-Au-1/20oz#	金币	普制	1/20	14	20	99.9	600000	深圳、上海
2011-0206-Au-1kg#	金币	精制	1公斤	90	10000	99.9	300	沈阳
2011-0207-Au-5oz#	金币	精制	5	60	2000	99.9	2000	沈阳
2011-0208-Ag-1kg#	银币	精制	1公斤	100	300	99.9	8000	沈阳
2011-0209-Ag-5oz#	银币	精制	5	70	50	99.9	20000	沈阳
2011-0210-Ag-1oz#	银币	普制	1	40	10	99.9	6000000	深圳、沈阳、上海

正面图案：北京天坛祈年殿

编码：2011-0206-Au-1kg#
背面图案：母子熊猫图

正面图案：
北京天坛祈年殿

编码：2011-0207-Au-5oz#
背面图案：母子熊猫图

正面图案：北京天坛祈年殿

2011版熊猫金银纪念币

2011 Chinese Panda Gold and Silver Commemorative Coins

编码：2011-0208-Ag-1kg#
背面图案：母子熊猫图

正面图案：北京天坛祈年殿

编码：2011-0209-Ag-5oz#
背面图案：母子熊猫图

正面图案：
北京天坛祈年殿

编码：2011-0210-Ag-1oz#
背面图案：母子熊猫图

新中国航空工业建立60周年熊猫加字金银纪念币

Panda Commemorative Gold and Silver Coins for the 60th Anniversary of Aviation Industry of P. R. China

正面图案：北京天坛祈年殿

编码：2011-0301-Au-1/4oz#
背面图案：母子熊猫图

新中国航空工业建立60周年熊猫加字金银纪念币

Panda Commemorative Gold and Silver Coins for the 60th Anniversary of Aviation Industry of P. R. China

正面图案：北京天坛祈年殿

编码：2011-0302-Ag-1oz#
背面图案：母子熊猫图

本套币正面图稿设计者：孙奇龄
正面浮雕制作者：岳俊峰
背面图稿设计者：赵　樯
背面浮雕制作者：宋　飞

金币1枚 银币1枚　1 Gold Coin 1 Silver Coin

编码	材质	质量	重量(盎司)	直径(毫米)	面额(元)	成色(%)	最大发行量(枚)	铸造单位
2011-0301-Au-1/4oz#	金币	普制	1/4	22	100	99.9	5000	深圳
2011-0302-Ag-1oz#	银币	普制	1	40	10	99.9	20000	深圳

2011西安世界园艺博览会熊猫加字金银纪念币

Panda Commemorative Gold and Silver Coins for the International Horticultural Exposition 2011 Xi'an China

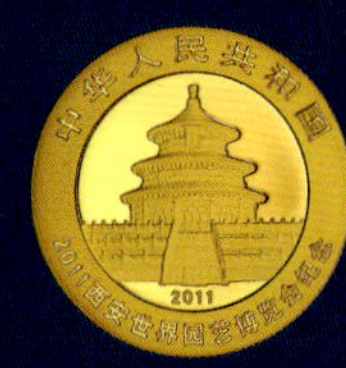

正面图案：北京天坛祈年殿

编码：2011-0501-Au-1/4oz#
背面图案：母子熊猫图

正面图案：北京天坛祈年殿

编码：2011-0502-Ag-1oz#
背面图案：母子熊猫图

本套币正面图稿设计者：孙奇龄
正面浮雕制作者：岳俊峰
背面图稿设计者：赵 樯
背面浮雕制作者：宋 飞

金币1枚 银币1枚 1 Gold Coin 1 Silver Coin

编码	材质	质量	重量(盎司)	直径(毫米)	面额(元)	成色(%)	最大发行量(枚)	铸造单位
2011-0501-Au-1/4oz#	金币	普制	1/4	22	100	99.9	3000	深圳
2011-0502-Ag-1oz#	银币	普制	1	40	10	99.9	20000	深圳

京沪高速铁路开通熊猫加字金银纪念币

Panda Commemorative Gold and Silver Coins for Beijing–Shanghai High Speed Rail Opening to Traffic

正面图案：北京天坛祈年殿

编码：2011-0701-Au-1/4oz#
背面图案：母子熊猫图

正面图案：北京天坛祈年殿

编码：2011-0702-Ag-1oz#
背面图案：母子熊猫图

本套币正面图稿设计者：孙奇龄
正面浮雕制作者：岳俊峰
背面图稿设计者：赵　樯
背面浮雕制作者：宋　飞

金币1枚 银币1枚　1 Gold Coin 1 Silver Coin

编码	材质	质量	重量(盎司)	直径(毫米)	面额(元)	成色(%)	最大发行量(枚)	铸造单位
2011-0701-Au-1/4zo#	金币	普制	1/4	22	100	99.9	10000	深圳
2011-0702-Ag-1oz#	银币	普制	1	40	10	99.9	30000	深圳

中国金融工会全国委员会成立60周年熊猫加字纪念银币

The Panda Commemorative Silver Coins for the 60th Anniversary of the National Committee of the Chinese Financial Workers' Union

正面图案：北京天坛祈年殿

编码：2011-1101-Ag-1oz#
背面图案：母子熊猫图

本套币正面图稿设计者：孙奇龄
正面浮雕制作者：岳俊峰
背面图稿设计者：赵　樯
背面浮雕制作者：宋　飞

银币1枚　1 Silver Coin

编码	材质	质量	重量(盎司)	直径(毫米)	面额(元)	成色(%)	最大发行量(枚)	铸造单位
2011-1101-Ag-1oz#	银币	普制	1	40	10	99.9	30000	深圳

上海黄金交易所成立10周年熊猫加字金银纪念币

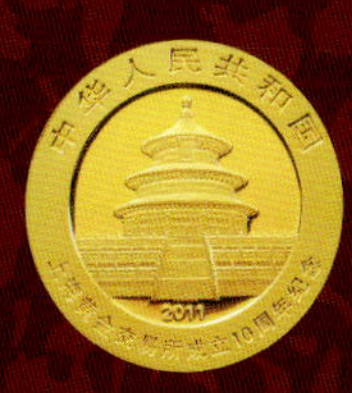

正面图案：北京天坛祈年殿

编码：2011-1501-Au-1/4oz#
背面图案：母子熊猫图

正面图案：北京天坛祈年殿

编码：2011-1502-Ag-1oz#
背面图案：母子熊猫图

本套币正面图稿设计者：孙奇龄
正面浮雕制作者：岳俊峰
背面图稿设计者：赵　樯
背面浮雕制作者：宋　飞

金币1枚 银币1枚　1 Gold Coin 1 Silver Coin

编码	材质	质量	重量(盎司)	直径(毫米)	面额(元)	成色(%)	最大发行量(枚)	铸造单位
2011-1501-Au-1/4oz#	金币	普制	1/4	22	100	99.9	6000	深圳
2011-1502-Ag-1oz#	银币	普制	1	40	10	99.9	30000	深圳

厦门经济特区建设30周年熊猫加字金银纪念币

Panda Commemorative Gold and Silver Coins for the 30th Anniversary of Xiamen Special Economic Zone

正面图案：北京天坛祈年殿

编码：2011-1701-Au-1/4oz#
背面图案：母子熊猫图

正面图案：北京天坛祈年殿

编码：2011-1702-Ag-1oz#
背面图案：母子熊猫图

本套币正面图稿设计者：孙奇龄
正面浮雕制作者：岳俊峰
背面图稿设计者：赵 樯
背面浮雕制作者：宋 飞

金币1枚 银币1枚 1 Gold Coin 1 Silver Coin

编码	材质	质量	重量(盎司)	直径(毫米)	面额(元)	成色(%)	最大发行量(枚)	铸造单位
2011-1701-Au-1/4oz#	金币	普制	1/4	22	100	99.9	5000	深圳
2011-1702-Ag-1oz#	银币	普制	1	40	10	99.9	20000	深圳

厦门经济特区建设30周年熊猫加字金银纪念币

Panda Commemorative Gold and Silver Coins for the 30th Anniversary of Xiamen Special Economic Zone

新中国农村信用社成立60周年熊猫加字金银纪念币

Panda Commemorative Gold and Silver Coins for the 60th Anniversary of the Rural Credit Cooperatives of P.R. China

正面图案：北京天坛祈年殿

编码：2011-1801-Au-1/4oz#
背面图案：母子熊猫图

正面图案：北京天坛祈年殿

编码：2011-1802-Ag-1oz#
背面图案：母子熊猫图

本套币正面图稿设计者：孙奇龄
正面浮雕制作者：岳俊峰
背面图稿设计者：赵　樯
背面浮雕制作者：宋　飞

金币1枚 银币1枚　1 Gold Coin 1 Silver Coin

编码	材质	质量	重量(盎司)	直泾(毫米)	面额(元)	成色(%)	最大发行量(枚)	铸造单位
2011-1801-Au-1/4oz#	金币	普制	1/4	22	100	99.9	25000	深圳
2011-1802-Ag-1oz#	银币	普制	1	40	10	99.9	60000	深圳

2011中国辛卯（兔）年金银纪念币

2011 Chinese Xin Mao Year (Year of the Rabbit) Gold and Silver Commemorative Coins

正面图案：中华人民共和国国徽及连年有余吉祥纹饰
设计者：张文静
浮雕制作者：集体

2011中国辛卯（兔）年金银纪念币

2011 Chinese Xin Mao Year (Year of the Rabbit) Gold and Silver Commemorative Coins

编码：2011-0101-Au-10kg
背面图案：兔及装饰兔首
设计者：朱熙华
浮雕制作者：宋飞

正面图案：中华人民共和国国徽及连年有余吉祥纹饰
设计者：张文静　浮雕制作者：集体

编码：2011-0102-Au-1kg
背面图案：兔及装饰兔首
设计者：朱熙华　浮雕制作者：宋飞

2011中国辛卯（兔）年金银纪念币

2011 Chinese Xin Mao Year (Year of the Rabbit) Gold and Silver Commemorative Coins

正面图案：中华人民共和国国徽及连年有
设计者：张文静
浮雕制作者：集体

编码：2011-0103-Au-5oz
背面图案：中国民间传统装饰兔图形及吉
设计者：张文静　何忠
浮雕制作者：张春晔

金币8枚　银币7枚　8 Gold Coins 7 Silver Coins

编码	材质	质量	重量(盎司)	形制尺寸(毫米)	面额(元)	成色(%)	最大发行量(枚)	铸造单位
2011-0101-Au-10kg	金币	精制	10公斤	圆形直径180	100000	99.9	18	深圳
2011-0102-Au-1kg	金币	精制	1公斤	梅花形外接圆直径100	10000	99.9	118	深圳
2011-0103-Au-5oz	彩色金币	精制	5	圆形直径60	2000	99.9	1800	上海
2011-0104-Au-5oz	金币	精制	5	长方形64×40	2000	99.9	118	上海
2011-0105-Au-1/2oz	金币	精制	1/2	梅花形外接圆直径27	200	99.9	8000	上海
2011-0106-Au-1/2oz	金币	普制	1/2	扇形外圆半径58,内圆半径39,圆心角30度	200	99.9	6600	深圳
2011-0107-Au-1/10oz	彩色金币	精制	1/10	圆形直径18	50	99.9	80000	上海
2011-0108-Au-1/10oz	金币	精制	1/10	圆形直径18	50	99.9	80000	沈阳
2011-0109-Ag-1kg	银币	精制	1公斤	圆形直径100	300	99.9	3800	沈阳
2011-0110-Ag-5oz	彩色银币	精制	5	圆形直径70	50	99.9	11800	上海
2011-0111-Ag-5oz	银币	精制	5	长方形80×50	50	99.9	1888	沈阳
2011-0112-Ag-1oz	彩色银币	精制	1	圆形直径40	10	99.9	220000	上海
2011-0113-Ag-1oz	银币	精制	1	梅花形外接圆直径40	10	99.9	60000	深圳
2011-0114-Ag-1oz	银币	普制	1	扇形外圆半径85,内圆半径60,圆心角30度	10	99.9	66000	沈阳
2011-0115-Ag-1oz	银币	精制	1	圆形直径40	10	99.9	180000	深圳

正面图案：中华人民共和国国徽及连年有余吉祥纹饰
设计者：张文静
浮雕制作者：集体

编码：2011-0104-Au-5oz
背面图案：兔及装饰兔首
设计者：朱熙华
浮雕制作者：宋飞

正面图案：中华人民共和国国徽及连年有余吉祥纹饰
设计者：张文静
浮雕制作者：集体

编码：2011-0105-Au-1/2oz
背面图案：兔及装饰兔首
设计者：朱熙华
浮雕制作者：宋飞

正面图案：甘肃嘉峪关
设计者：曾成沪
浮雕制作者：钟承辛

编码：2011-0106-Au-1/2oz
背面图案：兔及装饰兔首
设计者：朱熙华
浮雕制作者：宋飞

2011中国辛卯（兔）年金银纪念币

2011 Chinese Xin Mao Year (Year of the Rabbit) Gold and Silver Commemorative Coins

共同正面
正面图案：中华人民共和国国徽及连年有余吉祥纹饰
设计者：张文静
浮雕制作者：集体

编码：2011-0107-Au-1/10oz
背面图案：中国民间传统装饰兔图形及吉祥花卉
设计者：张文静　何忠
浮雕制作者：张春晔

编码：2011-0108-Au-1/10oz
背面图案：兔及装饰兔首
设计者：朱熙华
浮雕制作者：宋飞

正面图案：中华人民共和国国徽及连年有余吉祥纹饰
设计者：张文静　浮雕制作者：集体

编码：2011-0109-Ag-1kg
背面图案：兔及装饰兔首
设计者：朱熙华　浮雕制作者：宋飞

正面图案：中华人民共和国国徽
及连年有余吉祥纹饰
设计者：张文静　浮雕制作者：集体

编码：2011-0110-Ag-5oz
背面图案：中国民间传统装饰兔图形及吉祥花卉
设计者：张文静　何忠　浮雕制作者：张春晔

2011中国辛卯（兔）年金银纪念币

2011 Chinese Xin Mao Year (Year of the Rabbit) Gold and Silver Commemorative Coins

正面图案：中华人民共和国国徽及连年有余吉祥纹饰
设计者：张文静　浮雕制作者：集体

编码：2011-0111-Ag-5oz
背面图案：兔及装饰兔首
设计者：朱熙华　浮雕制作者：宋飞

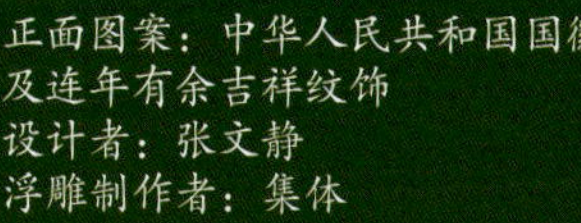

正面图案：中华人民共和国国徽
及连年有余吉祥纹饰
设计者：张文静
浮雕制作者：集体

编码：2011-0112-Ag-1oz
背面图案：中国民间传统装饰兔图形及吉祥花卉
设计者：张文静　何忠
浮雕制作者：张春晔

正面图案：中华人民共和国国徽
及连年有余吉祥纹饰
设计者：张文静
浮雕制作者：集体

编码：2011-0113-Ag-1oz
背面图案：兔及装饰兔首
设计者：朱熙华
浮雕制作者：宋飞

2011中国辛卯（兔）年金银纪念币

2011 Chinese Xin Mao Year (Year of the Rabbit) Gold and Silver Commemorative Coins

正面图案：甘肃嘉峪关
设计者：曾成沪
浮雕制作者：钟承辛

编码：2011-0114-Ag-1oz
背面图案：兔及装饰兔首
设计者：朱熙华
浮雕制作者：宋飞

正面图案：中华人民共和国国徽
及连年有余吉祥纹饰
设计者：张文静
浮雕制作者：集体

编码：2011-0115-Ag-1oz
背面图案：兔及装饰兔首
设计者：朱熙华
浮雕制作者：宋飞

中国京剧脸谱彩色金银纪念币（第2组）

Chinese Peking Opera Facial Mask Colored Commemorative Gold and Silver Coins (2nd Set)

正面图案：中华人民共和国国徽
及海水江牙、祥云
设计者：王虎鸣
浮雕制作者：黄喆　胥瑜婷

编码：2011-0401-Au-1/4oz
背面图案："关羽"京剧脸谱
设计者：王虎鸣
浮雕制作者：贵庆东

正面图案：中华人民共和国国徽
及海水江牙、祥云
设计者：王虎鸣
浮雕制作者：黄喆　胥瑜婷

编码：2011-0402-Ag-1oz
背面图案：鲁智深 京剧脸谱
设计者：王虎鸣
浮雕制作者：钟承辛

正面图案：中华人民共和国国徽
及海水江牙、祥云
设计者：王虎鸣
浮雕制作者：黄喆　胥瑜婷

编码：2011-0403-Ag-1oz
背面图案："单雄信"京剧脸谱
设计者：王虎鸣
浮雕制作者：禹飞

金币1枚　银币2枚　1 Gold Coin 2 Silver Coins

编码	材质	质量	重量(盎司)	直径(毫米)	面额(元)	成色(%)	最大发行量(枚)	铸造单位
2011-0401-Au-1/4oz	彩色金币	精制	1/4	22	100	99.9	30000	深圳
2011-0402-Ag-1oz	彩色银币	精制	1	40	10	99.9	50000	深圳
2011-0403-Ag-1oz	彩色银币	精制	1	40	10	99.9	50000	深圳

深圳第26届世界大学生夏季运动会金银纪念币

The Commemorative Gold and Silver Coins for the 26th Summer Universiade, Shenzhen

正面图案：深圳第26届世界大学生夏季运动会会徽
设计者：董慧珍
浮雕制作者：马光华

编码：2011-0601-Au-1/4oz
背面图案：深圳第26届世界大学生夏季运动会吉祥物及跑道、光束、繁星等
设计者：钟承辛　邓姗姗
浮雕制作者：谢欣锐

正面图案：深圳第26届世界大学生夏季运动会会徽
设计者：董慧珍
浮雕制作者：马光华

编码：2011-0602-Ag-1oz
背面图案：深圳第26届世界大学生夏季运动会“大运中心”及水中倒影
设计者：黄喆
浮雕制作者：邓姗姗

金币1枚　银币1枚　1 Gold Coin 1 Silver Coin

编码	材质	质量	重量(盎司)	直径(毫米)	面额(元)	成色(%)	最大发行量(枚)	铸造单位
2011-0601-Au-1/4oz	金币	精制	1/4	22	100	99.9	20000	上海
2011-0602-Ag-1oz	银币	精制	1	40	10	99.9	30000	深圳

世界自然基金会成立50周年金银纪念币

The Official Commemorative Gold and Silver Coins for the 50th Anniversary of the World Wide Fund for Nature (WWF)

正面图案：中华人民共和国国徽
设计者：中国金币总公司提供
浮雕制作者：集体

编码：2011-0801-Au-1/4oz
背面图案：数字"50"装饰造型与世界自然基金会（WWF）标识、地球
设计者：广州东方红文化策划传播有限公司
浮雕制作者：费庆东

编码：2011-0802-Ag-1oz
背面图案：藏羚羊及藏羚羊群、雪山装饰图形
设计者：朱熙华
浮雕制作者：邓姗姗

正面图案：中华人民共和国国徽
设计者：中国金币总公司提供
浮雕制作者：集体

金币1枚　银币1枚　1 Gold Coin 1 Silver Coin

编码	材质	质量	重量(盎司)	直泾(毫米)	面额(元)	成色(%)	最大发行量(枚)	铸造单位
2011-0801-Au-1/4oz	金币	精制	1/4	22	100	99.9	10000	深圳
2011-0802-Ag-1oz	银币	精制	1	40	10	99.9	30000	深圳

世界自然基金会成立50周年金银纪念币

The Official Commemorative Gold and Silver Coins for the 50th Anniversary of the World Wide Fund for Nature (WWF)

1911-2011
清華園
庆祝清华大学建校100周年大会
2011

正面图案：中华人民共和国国徽
设计者：中国金币总公司提供
浮雕制作者：集体

编码：2011-0901-Au-1/4oz
背面图案：清华大学建校100周年校庆标识
设计者：陶斯雯
浮雕制作者：魏雪飞

正面图案：中华人民共和国国徽
设计者：中国金币总公司提供
浮雕制作者：集体

清华大学建校100周年金银纪念币

The Official Commemorative Gold and Silver Coins for Tsinghua University Centenary Celebration

编码：2011-0902-Ag-1oz
背面图案：清华大学"二校门"
设计者：陶斯雯
浮雕制作者：禹飞

金币1枚 银币1枚 1 Gold Coin 1 Silver Coin

编码	材质	质量	重量(盎司)	直径(毫米)	面额(元)	成色(%)	最大发行量(枚)	铸造单位
2011-0901-Au-1/4oz	金币	精制	1/4	22	100	99.9	20000	深圳
2011-0902-Ag-1oz	银币	精制	1	40	10	99.9	50000	深圳

世界遗产——登封『天地之中』历史建筑群金银纪念币

The Official Commemorative Gold and Silver Coins of the Historical Monuments of Dengfeng in "the Centre of Heaven and Earth"

正面图案：中华人民共和国国徽
设计者：中国金币总公司提供
浮雕制作者：集体

编码：2011-1001-Au-1kg
背面图案：观星台、传统建筑斗拱及方位图、观星台建筑装饰图案
设计者：邱燕新
浮雕制作者：费庆东

正面图案：中华人民共和国国徽
设计者：中国金币总公司提供
浮雕制作者：集体

编码：2011-1002-Au-5oz
背面图案：太室阙、传统建筑斗拱及方位图、太室阙画像石装饰图案
设计者：邱燕新　浮雕制作者：宋飞

世界遗产——登封“天地之中”历史建筑群金银纪念币

The Official Commemorative Gold and Silver Coins of the Historical Monuments of Dengfeng in "the Centre of Heaven and Earth"

正面图案：中华人民共和国国徽
设计者：中国金币总公司提供
浮雕制作者：集体

编码：2011-1003-Au-1/4oz
背面图案：少林寺山门、传统建筑斗拱及方位图、少林寺建筑装饰图案
设计者：邱燕新　浮雕制作者：钟承辛

金币3枚　银币2枚　3 Gold Coins　2 Silver Coins

编码	材质	质量	重量(盎司)	直径(毫米)	面额(元)	成色(%)	最大发行量(枚)	铸造单位
2011-1001-Au-1kg	金币	精制	1公斤	90	10000	99.9	200	深圳
2011-1002-Au-5oz	金币	精制	5	60	2000	99.9	1000	深圳
2011-1003-Au-1/4oz	金币	精制	1/4	22	100	99.9	30000	深圳
2011-1004-Ag-1kg	银币	精制	1公斤	100	300	99.9	5000	深圳
2011-1005-Ag-1oz	银币	精制	1	40	10	99.9	60000	上海

正面图案：中华人民共和国国徽
设计者：中国金币总公司提供
浮雕制作者：集体

正面图案：中华人民共和国国徽
设计者：中国金币总公司提供
浮雕制作者：集体

编码：2011-1004-Ag-1kg
背面图案：中岳庙天中阁、传统建筑斗拱
及方位图、中岳庙建筑装饰图案
设计者：邱燕新
浮雕制作者：禹飞

编码：2011-1005-Ag-1oz
背面图案：嵩岳寺塔、传统建筑斗拱
及方位图、嵩岳寺塔建筑装饰图案
设计者：邱燕新
浮雕制作者：董慧珍

西藏和平解放60周年金银纪念币

The Commemorative Gold and Silver Coins for the 60th Anniversary of the Peaceful Liberation of Tibet

西藏和平解放60周年金银纪念币

The Commemorative Gold and Silver Coins for the 60th Anniversary of the Peaceful Liberation of Tibet

正面图案：中华人民共和国国徽
设计者：中国金币总公司提供
浮雕制作者：集体

编码：2011-1201-Au-1/4oz
背面图案：莲花、哈达及雪山、吉祥花草纹样
设计者：周剑
浮雕制作者：谢欣锐

正面图案：中华人民共和国国徽
设计者：中国金币总公司提供
浮雕制作者：集体

编码：2011-1202-Ag-1oz
背面图案：藏族传统吉祥图“八瑞相”及哈达、祥云纹样
设计者：周剑　浮雕制作者：董慧珍

金币1枚　银币1枚　1 Gold Coin 1 Silver Coin

编码	材质	质量	重量(盎司)	直径(毫米)	面额(元)	成色(%)	最大发行量(枚)	铸造单位
2011-1201-Au-1/4oz	金币	精制	1/4	22	100	99.9	20000	上海
2011-1202-Ag-1oz	银币	精制	1	40	10	99.9	30000	上海

辛亥革命100周年金银纪念币

The Commemorative Gold and Silver Coins for the 100th Anniversary of Xinhai Revolution

正面图案：中华人民共和国国徽
设计者：中国金币总公司提供
浮雕制作者：集体

编码：2011-1301-Au-1/4oz
背面图案：孙中山头像
设计者：中国金币总公司提供
浮雕制作者：韩晓生

正面图案：中华人民共和国国徽
设计者：中国金币总公司提供
浮雕制作者：集体

编码：2011-1302-Ag-1oz
背面图案："武昌起义"浮雕
设计者：陶峥
浮雕制作者：韩晓生

金币1枚 银币1枚　1 Gold Coin 1 Silver Coin

编码	材质	质量	重量(盎司)	直径(毫米)	面额(元)	成色(%)	最大发行量(枚)	铸造单位
2011-1301-Au-1/4oz	金币	精制	1/4	22	100	99.9	100000	沈阳
2011-1302-Ag-1oz	银币	精制	1	40	10	99.9	160000	沈阳

2011北京国际钱币博览会银质纪念币

2011 Beijing International Coin Exposition Commemorative Silver Coins

正面图案：象征钱币、地球的点线图案与2011北京国际钱币博览会会标
设计者：朱熙华
浮雕制作者：禹飞

编码：2011-1401-Ag-1oz
背面图案：中国宋代方孔圆钱与拜占庭希拉克略王朝钱币
设计者：齐云兰
浮雕制作者：蔡寅星

银币1枚 1 Silver Coin

编码	材质	质量	重量(盎司)	直径(毫米)	面额(元)	成色(%)	最大发行量(枚)	铸造单位
2011-1401-Ag-1oz	银币	精制	1	40	10	99.9	30000	上海

正面图案：中华人民共和国国徽及中国传统纹样
设计者：李继业
浮雕制作者：马光华

编码：2011-1601-Au-1kg
背面图案：齐聚忠义堂
设计者：宋鉴
浮雕制作者：钟承辛

正面图案：中华人民共和国国徽及中国传统纹样
设计者：李继业
浮雕制作者：马光华

编码：2011-1602-Au-5oz
背面图案：呼延灼月夜赚关胜
设计者：张磊
浮雕制作者：董慧珍

正面图案：中华人民共和国国徽及中国传统纹样
设计者：李继业
浮雕制作者：马光华

编码：2011-1603-Au-1/3oz
背面图案：吴用
设计者：张磊
浮雕制作者：魏雪飞

正面图案：中华人民共和国国徽及中国传统纹样
设计者：李继业
浮雕制作者：马光华

中国古典文学名著——《水浒传》彩色金银纪念币（第3组）

The Chinese Famous Classical Literature Works—*Outlaws of the Marsh*
Colored Gold and Silver Commemorative Coins (3rd Set)

编码：2011-1604-Ag-1kg
背面图案：齐聚忠义堂
设计者：宋鉴
浮雕制作者：钟承辛

金币3枚 银币4枚 3 Gold Coins 4 Silver Coins

编码	材质	质量	重量(盎司)	形制尺寸(毫米)	面额(元)	成色(%)	最大发行量(枚)	铸造单位
2011-1601-Au-1kg	彩色金币	精制	1公斤	圆形直径90	10000	99.9	200	深圳
2011-1602-Au-5oz	彩色金币	精制	5	长方形64×40	2000	99.9	900	上海
2011-1603-Au-1/3oz	彩色金币	精制	1/3	圆形直径23	150	99.9	35000	深圳
2011-1604-Ag-1kg	彩色银币	精制	1公斤	圆形直径100	300	99.9	10000	深圳
2011-1605-Ag-5oz	彩色银币	精制	5	长方形80×50	50	99.9	12000	上海
2011-1606-Ag-1oz	彩色银币	精制	1	圆形直径40	10	99.9	70000	上海
2011-1607-Ag-1oz	彩色银币	精制	1	圆形直径40	10	99.9	70000	沈阳

正面图案：中华人民共和国国徽及中国传统纹样
设计者：李继业
浮雕制作者：马光华

编码：2011-1605-Ag-5oz
背面图案：燕青智扑擎天柱
设计者：张磊
浮雕制作者：鲁丹叶

共同正面
正面图案：中华人民共和国国徽及中国传统纹样
设计者：李继业
浮雕制作者：马光华

编码：2011-1606-Ag-1oz
背面图案：小李广梁山射雁
设计者：张磊
浮雕制作者：上海造币有限公司

编码：2011-1607-Ag-1oz
背面图案：李逵探母
设计者：张磊
浮雕制作者：常欢　张文静

中国古典文学名著——《水浒传》彩色金银纪念币（第3组）

The Chinese Famous Classical Literature Works—*Outlaws of the Marsh* Colored Gold and Silver Commemorative Coins (3rd Set)

2012

2012版熊猫金银纪念币

2012 Chinese Panda Gold and Silver Commemorative Coins

中国熊猫金币发行30周年金银纪念币

The 30th Anniversary of the Issuance of Chinese Panda Gold Coin Gold and Silver Commemorative Coins

中国银行成立100周年熊猫加字金银纪念币

The 100th Anniversary of Bank of China Panda Gold and Silver Commemorative Coins

华夏银行成立20周年熊猫加字金银纪念币

The 20th Anniversary of Hua Xia Bank Panda Gold and Silver Commemorative Coins

招商银行成立25周年暨上市10周年熊猫加字金银纪念币

The 25th Anniversary of the Founding and 10th Anniversary of Listing of China Merchants Bank Panda Gold and Silver Commemorative Coins

2012中国壬辰（龙）年金银纪念币

2012 Chinese Ren Chen Year (Year of the Dragon) Gold and Silver Commemorative Coins

中国佛教圣地（五台山）金银纪念币

Chinese Sacred Buddhist Mountain (Mount Wutai) Gold and Silver Commemorative Coins

中国京剧脸谱彩色金银纪念币（第3组）

Chinese Peking Opera Facial Mask Colored Gold and Silver Commemorative Coins (3rd set)

中国青铜器金银纪念币（第1组）

The Chinese Bronze Ware Gold and Silver Commemorative Coins (1st Issue)

2012北京国际邮票钱币博览会银质纪念币

The Commemorative Silver Coin for Beijing International Stamp and Coin Exposition 2012

中国人民解放军海军航母辽宁舰金银纪念币

The PLA Navy Aircraft Carrier "Liaoning" Gold and Silver Commemorative Coins

2012版熊猫金银纪念币

2012 Chinese Panda Gold and Silver Commemorative Coins

中国熊猫金币发行30周年金银纪念币

The 30th Anniversary of the Issuance of Chinese Panda Gold Coin Gold and Silver Commemorative Coins

中国银行成立100周年熊猫加字金银纪念币

The 100th Anniversary of Bank of China Panda Gold and Silver Commemorative Coins

华夏银行成立20周年熊猫加字金银纪念币

The 20th Anniversary of Hua Xia Bank Panda Gold and Silver Commemorative Coins

招商银行成立25周年暨上市10周年熊猫加字金银纪念币

The 25th Anniversary of the Founding and 10th Anniversary of Listing of China Merchants Bank Panda Gold and Silver Commemorative Coins

2012中国壬辰（龙）年金银纪念币

2012 Chinese Ren Chen Year (Year of the Dragon) Gold and Silver Commemorative Coins

中国佛教圣地（五台山）金银纪念币

Chinese Sacred Buddhist Mountain (Mount Wutai) Gold and Silver Commemorative Coins

中国京剧脸谱彩色金银纪念币（第3组）

Chinese Peking Opera Facial Mask Colored Gold and Silver Commemorative Coins (3rd set)

中国青铜器金银纪念币（第1组）

The Chinese Bronze Ware Gold and Silver Commemorative Coins (1st Issue)

2012北京国际邮票钱币博览会银质纪念币

The Commemorative Silver Coin for Beijing International Stamp and Coin Exposition 2012

中国人民解放军海军航母辽宁舰金银纪念币

The PLA Navy Aircraft Carrier "Liaoning" Gold and Silver Commemorative Coins

2012版熊猫金银纪念币

2012 Chinese Panda Gold and Silver Commemorative Coins

共同正面
正面图案：北京天坛祈年殿

编码：2012-0201-Au-1oz#
背面图案：母子熊猫图

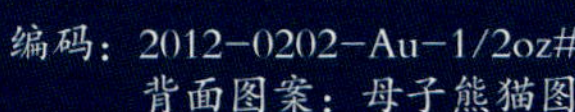

编码：2012-0202-Au-1/2oz#
背面图案：母子熊猫图

编码：2012-0203-Au-1/4oz#
背面图案：母子熊猫图

编码：2012-0204-Au-1/10oz#
背面图案：母子熊猫图

编码：2012-0205-Au-1/20oz#
背面图案：母子熊猫图

本套币正面图稿设计者：孙奇龄
正面浮雕制作者：岳俊峰
背面图稿设计者：程　超
背面浮雕制作者：余　敏

金币7枚 银币3枚　7 Gold Coins 3 Silver Coins

编码	材质	质量	重量(盎司)	直径(毫米)	面额(元)	成色(%)	最大发行量(枚)	铸造单位
2012-0201-Au-1oz#	金币	普制	1	32	500	99.9	600000	上海、沈阳、深圳
2012-0202-Au-1/2oz#	金币	普制	1/2	27	200	99.9	600000	上海、沈阳、深圳
2012-0203-Au-1/4oz#	金币	普制	1/4	22	100	99.9	600000	上海、沈阳、深圳
2012-0204-Au-1/10oz#	金币	普制	1/10	18	50	99.9	800000	上海、沈阳、深圳
2012-0205-Au-1/20oz#	金币	普制	1/20	14	20	99.9	800000	上海、沈阳、深圳
2012-0206-Au-1kg#	金币	精制	1公斤	90	10000	99.9	500	沈阳
2012-0207-Au-5oz#	金币	精制	5	60	2000	99.9	5000	沈阳
2012-0208-Ag-1kg#	银币	精制	1公斤	100	300	99.9	20000	沈阳
2012-0209-Ag-5oz#	银币	精制	5	70	50	99.9	50000	沈阳
2012-0210-Ag-1oz#	银币	普制	1	40	10	99.9	8000000	上海、沈阳、深圳

共同正面
正面图案：北京天坛祈年殿

编码：2012-0206-Au-1kg#
背面图案：母子熊猫图

编码：2012-0207-Au-5oz#
背面图案：母子熊猫图

共同正面
正面图案：北京天坛祈年殿

编码：2012-0208-Ag-1kg#
背面图案：母子熊猫图

编码：2012-0209-Ag-5oz#
背面图案：母子熊猫图

正面图案：
北京天坛祈年殿

编码：2012-0210-Ag-1oz#
背面图案：母子熊猫图

共同正面
正面图案：北京天坛祈年殿
设计者：孙奇龄　浮雕制作者：岳俊峰

编码：2012-0301-Au-5oz#
背面图案：熊猫及长城、竹子
设计者：常欢　浮雕制作者：邓姗姗

编码：2012-0302-Au-1oz#
背面图案：熊猫及竹林
设计者：谷克沙　浮雕制作者：王文栋

编码：2012-0303-Au-1/10oz#
背面图案：熊猫及竹林、倒影
设计者：王刚　浮雕制作者：王刚

共同正面
正面图案：北京天坛祈年殿
设计者：孙奇龄　浮雕制作者：岳俊峰

编码：2012-0304-Ag-5oz#
背面图案：熊猫及竹子、山石
设计者：谷英斌　浮雕制作者：余敏

编码：2012-0305-Ag-1/4oz#
背面图案：代表“30”的卡通熊猫图及竹叶
设计者：余敏　浮雕制作者：费庆东

金币3枚　银币2枚　3 Gold Coins　2 Silver Coins

编码	材质	质量	重量(盎司)	直径(毫米)	面额(元)	成色(%)	最大发行量(枚)	铸造单位
2012-0301-Au-5oz#	金币	精制	5	60	2000	99.9	3000	深圳
2012-0302-Au-1oz#	金币	精制	1	32	500	99.9	30000	上海
2012-0303-Au-1/10oz#	金币	精制	1/10	18	50	99.9	100000	沈阳
2012-0304-Ag-5oz#	银币	精制	5	70	50	99.9	30000	上海
2012-0305-Ag-1/4oz#	银币	精制	1/4	25	3	99.9	300000	深圳

中国熊猫金币发行30周年金银纪念币

The 30th Anniversary of the Issuance of Chinese Panda Gold Coin Gold and Silver Commemorative Coins

中国银行
BANK OF CHINA

正面图案：北京天坛祈年殿

编码：2012-0401-Au-1/4oz#
背面图案：母子熊猫图

中国银行成立100周年熊猫加字金银纪念币

The 100th Anniversary of Bank of China Panda Gold and Silver Commemorative Coins

正面图案：北京天坛祈年殿

编码：2012-0402-Ag-1oz#
背面图案：母子熊猫图

本套币正面图稿设计者：孙奇龄
正面浮雕制作者：岳俊峰
背面图稿设计者：程　超
背面浮雕制作者：余　敏

金币1枚 银币1枚　1 Gold Coin 1 Silver Coin

编码	材质	质量	重量(盎司)	直径(毫米)	面额(元)	成色(%)	最大发行量(枚)	铸造单位
2012-0401-Au-1/4oz#	金币	普制	1/4	22	100	99.9	55000	深圳
2012-0402-Ag-1oz#	银币	普制	1	40	10	99.9	260000	深圳

华夏银行成立20周年熊猫加字金银纪念币

The 20th Anniversary of Hua Xia Bank Panda Gold and Silver Commemorative Coins

正面图案：北京天坛祈年殿

编码：2012-0901-Au-1/4oz#
背面图案：母子熊猫图

正面图案：北京天坛祈年殿

编码：2012-0902-Ag-1oz#
背面图案：母子熊猫图

本套币正面图稿设计者：孙奇龄
正面浮雕制作者：岳俊峰
背面图稿设计者：程　超
背面浮雕制作者：余　敏

金币1枚 银币1枚　1 Gold Coin 1 Silver Coin

编码	材质	质量	重量(盎司)	直径(毫米)	面额(元)	成色(%)	最大发行量(枚)	铸造单位
2012-0901-Au-1/4oz#	金币	普制	1/4	22	100	99.9	10000	深圳
2012-0902-Ag-1oz#	银币	普制	1	40	10	99.9	50000	深圳

招商银行成立25周年暨上市10周年熊猫加字金银纪念币

The 25th Anniversary of the Founding and 10th Anniversary of Listing of China Merchants Bank Panda Gold and Silver Commemorative Coins

正面图案：北京天坛祈年殿

编码：2012-1001-Au-1/4oz#
背面图案：母子熊猫图

正面图案：北京天坛祈年殿

编码：2012-1002-Ag-1oz#
背面图案：母子熊猫图

本套币正面图稿设计者：孙奇龄
正面浮雕制作者：岳俊峰
背面图稿设计者：程　超
背面浮雕制作者：余　敏

金币1枚 银币1枚　1 Gold Coin 1 Silver Coin

编码	材质	质量	重量(盎司)	直泾(毫米)	面额(元)	成色(%)	最大发行量(枚)	铸造单位
2012-1001-Au-1/4oz#	金币	普制	1/4	22	100	99.9	20000	深圳
2012-1002-Ag-1oz#	银币	普制	1	40	10	99.9	30000	深圳

2012中国壬辰（龙）年金银纪念币

2012 Chinese Ren Chen Year (Year of the Dragon) Gold and Silver Commemorative Coins

正面图案：中华人民共和国国徽及连年有余吉祥纹饰
设计者：张文静
浮雕制作者：集体

2012中国壬辰（龙）年金银纪念币

2012 Chinese Ren Chen Year (Year of the Dragon) Gold and Silver Commemorative Coins

编码：2012-0101-Au-10kg
背面图案：青龙图及装饰龙头
设计者：朱熙华
浮雕制作者：宋飞

正面图案：中华人民共和国国徽及连年有余吉祥纹饰
设计者：张文静
浮雕制作者：集体

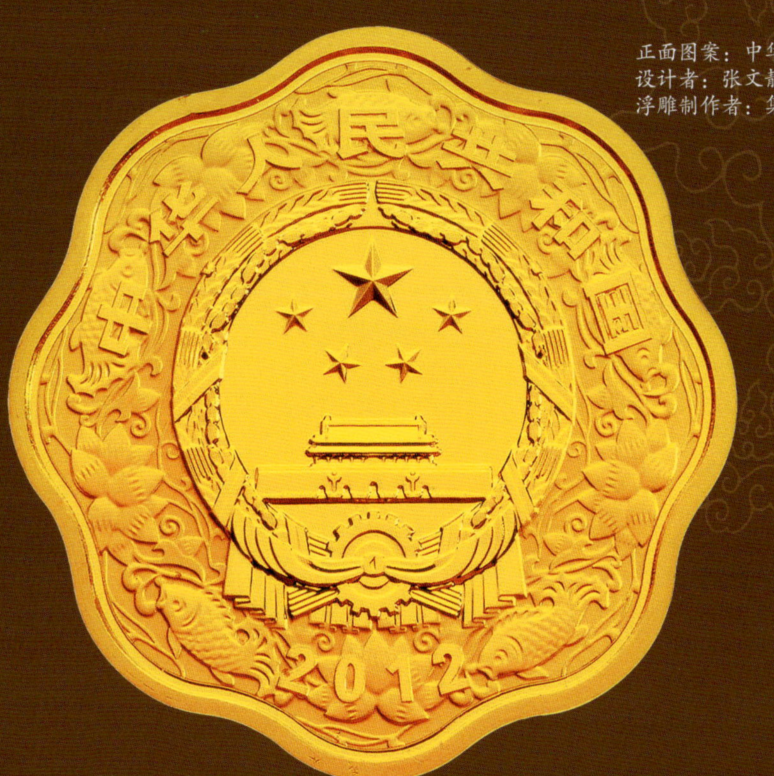

2012中国壬辰（龙）年金银纪念币

2012 Chinese Ren Chen Year (Year of the Dragon) Gold and Silver Commemorative Coins

编码：2012-0102-Au-1kg
背面图案：青龙图及装饰龙头
设计者：朱熙华
浮雕制作者：宋飞

正面图案：中华人民共和国国徽及连年有余吉祥纹饰
设计者：张文静
浮雕制作者：集体

编码：2012-0103-Au-5oz
背面图案：中国民间传统装饰龙图形及吉祥纹饰
设计者：张文静　何忠　何洁
浮雕制作者：张春晔

金币8枚　银币7枚　8 Gold Coins　7 Silver Coins

编码	材质	质量	重量(盎司)	形制尺寸(毫米)	面额(元)	成色(%)	最大发行量(枚)	铸造单位
2012-0101-Au-10kg	金币	精制	10公斤	圆形直径180	100000	99.9	18	深圳
2012-0102-Au-1kg	金币	精制	1公斤	梅花形外接圆直径100	10000	99.9	118	上海
2012-0103-Au-5oz	彩色金币	精制	5	圆形直径60	2000	99.9	3000	上海
2012-0104-Au-5oz	金币	精制	5	长方形64×40	2000	99.9	2000	沈阳
2012-0105-Au-1/2oz	金币	精制	1/2	梅花形外接圆直径27	200	99.9	8000	上海
2012-0106-Au-1/3oz	金币	精制	1/3	扇形外圆半径51，内圆半径36，圆心角30度	150	99.9	30000	深圳
2012-0107-Au-1/10oz	彩色金币	精制	1/10	圆形直径18	50	99.9	120000	沈阳
2012-0108-Au-1/10oz	金币	精制	1/10	圆形直径18	50	99.9	120000	沈阳
2012-0109-Ag-1kg	银币	精制	1公斤	圆形直径100	300	99.9	3800	深圳
2012-0110-Ag-5oz	彩色银币	精制	5	圆形直径70	50	99.9	30000	沈阳
2012-0111-Ag-5oz	银币	精制	5	长方形80×50	50	99.9	20000	上海
2012-0112-Ag-1oz	彩色银币	精制	1	圆形直径40	10	99.9	220000	沈阳
2012-0113-Ag-1oz	银币	精制	1	梅花形外接圆直径40	10	99.9	60000	上海
2012-0114-Ag-1oz	银币	精制	1	扇形外圆半径85，内圆半径60，圆心角30度	10	99.9	80000	深圳
2012-0115-Ag-1oz	银币	精制	1	圆形直径40	10	99.9	200000	上海

正面图案：中华人民共和国国徽及连年有余吉祥纹饰
设计者：张文静
浮雕制作者：集体

编码：2012-0104-Au-5oz
背面图案：青龙图及装饰龙头
设计者：朱熙华
浮雕制作者：宋飞

正面图案：中华人民共和国国徽及连年有余吉祥纹饰
设计者：张文静
浮雕制作者：集体

编码：2012-0105-Au-1/2oz
背面图案：青龙图及装饰龙头
设计者：朱熙华
浮雕制作者：宋飞

2012中国壬辰（龙）年金银纪念币

2012 Chinese Ren Chen Year (Year of the Dragon) Gold and Silver Commemorative Coins

正面图案：中华人民共和国国徽及连年有余吉祥纹饰
设计者：张文静
浮雕制作者：集体

编码：2012-0106-Au-1/3oz
背面图案：青龙图及装饰龙头
设计者：朱熙华
浮雕制作者：宋飞

共同正面
正面图案：中华人民共和国国徽及连年有余吉祥纹饰
设计者：张文静
浮雕制作者：集体

编码：2012-0107-Au-1/10oz
背面图案：中国民间传统装饰龙图形及吉祥纹饰
设计者：张文静　何忠　何洁
浮雕制作者：富丽莉

编码：2012-0108-Au-1/10oz
背面图案：青龙图及装饰龙头
设计者：朱熙华
浮雕制作者：宋飞

正面图案：中华人民共和国国徽及连年有余吉祥纹饰
设计者：张文静　浮雕制作者：集体

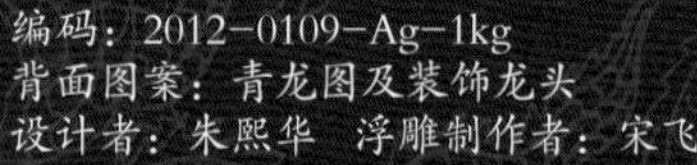

编码：2012-0109-Ag-1kg
背面图案：青龙图及装饰龙头
设计者：朱熙华　浮雕制作者：宋飞

正面图案：中华人民共和国国徽及连年有余吉祥纹饰
设计者：张文静　浮雕制作者：集体

编码：2012-0110-Ag-5oz
背面图案：中国民间传统装饰龙图形及吉祥纹饰
设计者：张文静　何忠　何洁　浮雕制作者：富丽莉

2012中国壬辰（龙）年金银纪念币

2012 Chinese Ren Chen Year (Year of the Dragon) Gold and Silver Commemorative Coins

正面图案：中华人民共和国国徽及连年有余吉祥纹饰
设计者：张文静　浮雕制作者：集体

编码：2012-0111-Ag-5oz
背面图案：青龙图及装饰龙头
设计者：朱熙华　浮雕制作者：宋飞

正面图案：中华人民共和国国徽
及连年有余吉祥纹饰
设计者：张文静
浮雕制作者：集体

编码：2012-0112-Ag-1oz
背面图案：中国民间传统装饰龙图形及吉祥纹饰
设计者：张文静　何忠　何洁
浮雕制作者：富丽莉

正面图案：中华人民共和国国徽
及连年有余吉祥纹饰
设计者：张文静
浮雕制作者：集体

编码：2012-0113-Ag-1oz
背面图案：青龙图及装饰龙头
设计者：朱熙华
浮雕制作者：宋飞

正面图案：中华人民共和国国徽
及连年有余吉祥纹饰
设计者：张文静
浮雕制作者：集体

编码：2012-0114-Ag-1oz
背面图案：青龙图及装饰龙头
设计者：朱熙华
浮雕制作者：宋飞

正面图案：中华人民共和国国徽
及连年有余吉祥纹饰
设计者：张文静
浮雕制作者：集体

编码：2012-0115-Ag-1oz
背面图案：青龙图及装饰龙头
设计者：朱熙华
浮雕制作者：宋飞

2012中国壬辰（龙）年金银纪念币

2012 Chinese Ren Chen Year (Year of the Dragon) Gold and Silver Commemorative Coins

正面图案：中华人民共和国国徽
设计者：中国金币总公司提供
浮雕制作者：集体

中国佛教圣地（五台山）金银纪念币

Chinese Sacred Buddhist Mountain (Mount Wutai) Gold and Silver Commemorative Coins

编码：2012-0501-Au-1kg
背面图案：佛光寺
设计者：王云野
浮雕制作者：鲁丹叶

正面图案：中华人民共和国国徽
设计者：中国金币总公司提供
浮雕制作者：集体

编码：2012-0502-Au-5oz
背面图案：显通寺
设计者：齐云兰
浮雕制作者：禹飞

正面图案：中华人民共和国国徽
设计者：中国金币总公司提供
浮雕制作者：集体

编码：2012-0503-Au-1/4oz
背面图案：菩萨顶
设计者：白牧
浮雕制作者：张春晔

金币3枚 银币2枚 3 Gold Coins 2 Silver Coins

编码	材质	质量	重量(盎司)	直径(毫米)	面额(元)	成色(%)	最大发行量(枚)	铸造单位
2012-0501-Au-1kg	金币	精制	1公斤	90	10000	99.9	300	上海
2012-0502-Au-5oz	金币	精制	5	60	2000	99.9	3000	深圳
2012-0503-Au-1/4oz	金币	精制	1/4	22	100	99.9	60000	上海
2012-0504-Ag-1kg	银币	精制	1公斤	100	300	99.9	10000	深圳
2012-0505-Ag-2oz	银币	精制	2	40	20	99.9	100000	深圳

共同正面
正面图案：中华人民共和国国徽
设计者：中国金币总公司提供
浮雕制作者：集体

编码：2012-0505-Ag-2oz
背面图案：文殊菩萨造像
设计者：宋飞
浮雕制作者：宋飞

中国佛教圣地（五台山）金银纪念币

Chinese Sacred Buddhist Mountain (Mount Wutai) Gold and Silver Commemorative Coins

编码：2012-0504-Ag-1kg
背面图案：塔院寺
设计者：宋飞　白牧
浮雕制作者：费庆东

中国京剧脸谱彩色金银纪念币（第3组）

Chinese Peking Opera Facial Mask Colored Gold and Silver Commemorative Coins (3rd set)

正面图案：中华人民共和国国徽及海水江牙、祥云
设计者：王虎鸣
浮雕制作者：黄喆　胥瑜婷

编码：2012-0601-Au-5oz
背面图案："关羽"京剧脸谱
设计者：王虎鸣
浮雕制作者：张磊

金币2枚　银币3枚　2 Gold Coins 3 Silver Coins

编码	材质	质量	重量(盎司)	直径(毫米)	面额(元)	成色(%)	最大发行量(枚)	铸造单位
2012-0601-Au-5oz	彩色金币	精制	5	60	2000	99.9	2000	深圳
2012-0602-Au-1/4oz	彩色金币	精制	1/4	22	100	99.9	30000	上海
2012-0603-Ag-5oz	彩色银币	精制	5	70	50	99.9	10000	上海
2012-0604-Ag-1oz	彩色银币	精制	1	40	10	99.9	50000	深圳
2012-0605-Ag-1oz	彩色银币	精制	1	40	10	99.9	50000	沈阳

正面图案：中华人民共和国国徽
及海水江牙、祥云
设计者：王虎鸣
浮雕制作者：黄喆　胥瑜婷

编码：2012－0602－Au－1/4oz
背面图案：“孙悟空”京剧脸谱
设计者：王虎鸣
浮雕制作者：朱熙华

正面图案：中华人民共和国国徽及海水江牙、祥云
设计者：王虎鸣
浮雕制作者：黄喆　胥瑜婷

中国京剧脸谱彩色金银纪念币（第3组）

Chinese Peking Opera Facial Mask Colored Gold and Silver Commemorative Coins (3rd set)

编码：2012－0603－Ag－5oz
背面图案：“钟馗”京剧脸谱
设计者：王虎鸣
浮雕制作者：全剑锋

正面图案：中华人民共和国国徽
设计者：中国金币总公司提供
浮雕制作者：集体

中国青铜器金银纪念币（第1组）

The Chinese Bronze Ware Gold and Silver Commemorative Coins (1st Issue)

编码：2012-0701-Au-5oz
背面图案：商代兽面纹方鼎
设计者：朱熙华
浮雕制作者：徐云飞

正面图案：中华人民共和国国徽
设计者：中国金币总公司提供
浮雕制作者：集体

编码：2012-0702-Au-1/4oz
背面图案：夏代乳钉纹爵
设计者：朱熙华
浮雕制作者：贲庆东

金币2枚 银币3枚　2 Gold Coins 3 Silver Coins

编码	材质	质量	重量(盎司)	直径(毫米)	面额(元)	成色(%)	最大发行量(枚)	铸造单位
2012-0701-Au-5oz	金币	精制	5	60	2000	99.9	2000	深圳
2012-0702-Au-1/4oz	金币	精制	1/4	22	100	99.9	50000	深圳
2012-0703-Ag-1kg	银币	精制	1公斤	100	300	99.9	6000	上海
2012-0704-Ag-5oz	银币	精制	5	70	50	99.9	10000	上海
2012-0705-Ag-1oz	银币	精制	1	40	10	99.9	80000	沈阳

正面图案：中华人民共和国国徽
设计者：中国金币总公司提供
浮雕制作者：集体

编码：2012-0703-Ag-1kg
背面图案：商代兽面纹斝
设计者：朱熙华
浮雕制作者：周卓

正面图案：中华人民共和国国徽
设计者：中国金币总公司提供
浮雕制作者：集体

编码：2012-0704-Ag-5oz
背面图案：商代兽面纹鬲
设计者：朱熙华
浮雕制作者：禹飞

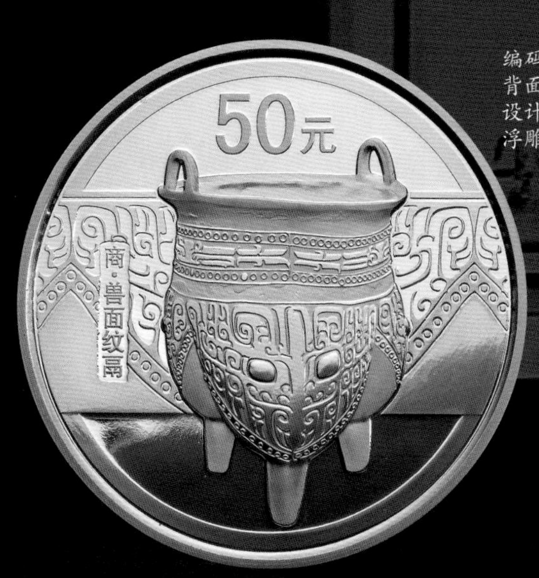

中国青铜器金银纪念币（第1组）

The Chinese Bronze Ware Gold and Silver Commemorative Coins (1st Issue)

正面图案：中华人民共和国国徽
设计者：中国金币总公司提供
浮雕制作者：集体

编码：2012-0705-Ag-1oz
背面图案：商代弦纹盉
设计者：朱熙华
浮雕制作者：邓姗姗

2012北京国际邮票钱币博览会银质纪念币

The Commemorative Silver Coin for Beijing International Stamp and Coin Exposition 2012

正面图案：象征钱币的圆点和装饰线与2012北京国际邮票钱币博览会会标
设计者：朱熙华
浮雕制作者：马光华

编码：2012-0801-Ag-1oz
背面图案：中国元代钱币与威尼斯公国钱币
设计者：齐云兰
浮雕制作者：张磊

银币1枚　1 Silver Coin

编码	材质	质量	重量(盎司)	直径(毫米)	面额(元)	成色(%)	最大发行量(枚)	铸造单位
2012-0801-Ag-1oz	银币	精制	1	40	10	99.9	30000	深圳

2012北京国际邮票钱币博览会银质纪念币

The Commemorative Silver Coin for Beijing International Stamp and Coin Exposition 2012

中国人民解放军海军航母辽宁舰金银纪念币
The PLA Navy Aircraft Carrier "Liaoning" Gold and Silver Commemorative Coi

正面图案：中华人民共和国国徽
设计者：中国金币总公司提供
浮雕制作者：集体

中国人民解放军海军航母辽宁舰金银纪念币

The PLA Navy Aircraft Carrier "Liaoning" Gold and Silver Commemorative Coins

编码：2012−1101−Au−5oz
背面图案：航母辽宁舰及海军臂章、航母甲板、舰载机
设计者：朱熙华
浮雕制作者：金雅轩

金币2枚 银币2枚　2 Gold Coins 2 Silver Coins

编码	材质	质量	重量(盎司)	直径(毫米)	面额(元)	成色(%)	最大发行量(枚)	铸造单位
2012−1101−Au−5oz	金币	精制	5	60	2000	99.9	2000	沈阳
2012−1102−Au−1/4oz	金币	精制	1/4	22	100	99.9	20000	沈阳
2012−1103−Ag−1kg	银币	精制	1公斤	100	300	99.9	3000	沈阳
2012−1104−Ag−1oz	银币	精制	1	40	10	99.9	50000	沈阳

正面图案：中华人民共和国国徽
设计者：中国金币总公司提供
浮雕制作者：集体

编码：2012-1102-Au-1/4oz
背面图案：航母辽宁舰及航母甲板、舰载机
设计者：邱燕新
浮雕制作者：常欢　富丽莉

正面图案：中华人民共和国国徽
设计者：中国金币总公司提供
浮雕制作者：集体

编码：2012-1104-Ag-1oz
背面图案：航母辽宁舰及航母甲板、舰载机
设计者：朱熙华
浮雕制作者：王刚

正面图案：中华人民共和国国徽
设计者：中国金币总公司提供
浮雕制作者：集体

中国人民解放军海军航母辽宁舰金银纪念币

The PLA Navy Aircraft Carrier "Liaoning" Gold and Silver Commemorative Coins

编码：2012-1103-Ag-1kg
背面图案：航母辽宁舰
及海军胸标、橄榄枝、和平鸽、地球
设计者：朱熙华
浮雕制作者：常欢　富丽莉

2013

2013版熊猫金银纪念币

2013 Chinese Panda Gold and Silver Commemorative Coins

上海浦东发展银行成立20周年熊猫加字金银纪念币

The 20th Anniversary of Shanghai Pudong Development Bank Panda Gold and Silver Commemorative Coins

中国光大集团成立30周年熊猫加字金银纪念币

The 30th Anniversary of China Everbright Group Panda Gold and Silver Commemorative Coins

中国—东盟博览会10周年熊猫加字金银纪念币

The 10th Anniversary of China-ASEAN Exposition Panda Gold and Silver Commemorative Coins

2013中国癸巳（蛇）年金银纪念币

2013 Chinese Gui Si Year (Year of the Snake) Gold and Silver Commemorative Coins

北斗卫星导航系统开通运行金银纪念币

Gold and Silver Commemorative Coins for the Start of the Operation of Compass Navigation Satellite System

中国佛教圣地（普陀山）金银纪念币

Chinese Sacred Buddhist Mountain (Mount Putuo) Gold and Silver Commemorative Coins

中国青铜器金银纪念币（第2组）

The Chinese Bronze Ware Gold and Silver Commemorative Coins (2nd Issue)

世界遗产——黄山金银纪念币

World Heritage—Huangshan Mountain Gold and Silver Commemorative Coins

2013北京国际钱币博览会银质纪念币

The Commemorative Silver Coin for Beijing International Coin Exposition 2013

2013版熊猫金银纪念币

2013 Chinese Panda Gold and Silver Commemorative Coins

上海浦东发展银行成立20周年熊猫加字金银纪念币

The 20th Anniversary of Shanghai Pudong Development Bank Panda Gold and Silver Commemorative Coins

中国光大集团成立30周年熊猫加字金银纪念币

The 30th Anniversary of China Everbright Group Panda Gold and Silver Commemorative Coins

中国—东盟博览会10周年熊猫加字金银纪念币

The 10th Anniversary of China-ASEAN Exposition Panda Gold and Silver Commemorative Coins

2013中国癸巳（蛇）年金银纪念币

2013 Chinese Gui Si Year (Year of the Snake) Gold and Silver Commemorative Coins

北斗卫星导航系统开通运行金银纪念币

Gold and Silver Commemorative Coins for the Start of the Operation of Compass Navigation Satellite System

中国佛教圣地（普陀山）金银纪念币

Chinese Sacred Buddhist Mountain (Mount Putuo) Gold and Silver Commemorative Coins

中国青铜器金银纪念币（第2组）

The Chinese Bronze Ware Gold and Silver Commemorative Coins (2nd Issue)

世界遗产——黄山金银纪念币

World Heritage – Huangshan Mountain Gold and Silver Commemorative Coins

2013北京国际钱币博览会银质纪念币

The Commemorative Silver Coin for Beijing International Coin Exposition 2013

2013版熊猫金银纪念币

2013 Chinese Panda Gold and Silver Commemorative Coins

共同正面
正面图案：北京天坛祈年殿

编码：2013-0201-Au-1oz#
背面图案：熊猫饮水图

编码：2013-0202-Au-1/2oz#
背面图案：熊猫饮水图

编码：2013-0203-Au-1/4oz#
背面图案：熊猫饮水图

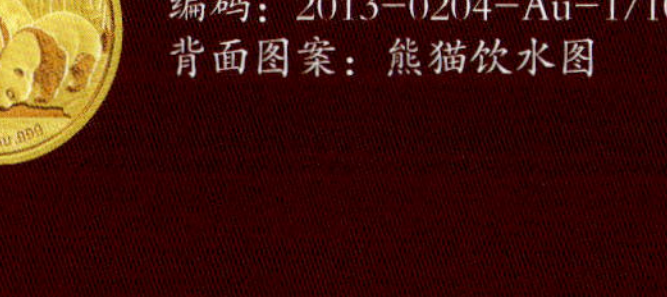

编码：2013-0204-Au-1/10oz#
背面图案：熊猫饮水图

编码：2013-0205-Au-1/20oz#
背面图案：熊猫饮水图

本套币正面图稿设计者：孙奇龄
正面浮雕制作者：岳俊峰
背面图稿设计者：程　超
背面浮雕制作者：余　敏

金币7枚　银币3枚　7 Gold Coins 3 Silver Coins

编码	材质	质量	重量(盎司)	直泾(毫米)	面额(元)	成色(%)	最大发行量(枚)	铸造单位
2013-0201-Au-1oz#	金币	普制	1	32	500	99.9	600000	上海、沈阳、深圳
2013-0202-Au-1/2oz#	金币	普制	1/2	27	200	99.9	600000	上海、沈阳、深圳
2013-0203-Au-1/4oz#	金币	普制	1/4	22	100	99.9	600000	上海、沈阳、深圳
2013-0204-Au-1/10oz#	金币	普制	1/10	18	50	99.9	800000	上海、沈阳、深圳
2013-0205-Au-1/20oz#	金币	普制	1/20	14	20	99.9	800000	上海、沈阳、深圳
2013-0206-Au-1kg#	金币	精制	1公斤	90	10000	99.9	500	沈阳
2013-0207-Au-5oz#	金币	精制	5	60	2000	99.9	5000	沈阳
2013-0208-Ag-1kg#	银币	精制	1公斤	100	300	99.9	20000	沈阳
2013-0209-Ag-5oz#	银币	精制	5	70	50	99.9	50000	沈阳
2013-0210-Ag-1oz#	银币	普制	1	40	10	99.9	8000000	上海、沈阳、深圳

共同正面
正面图案：北京天坛祈年殿

编码：2013-0206-Au-1kg#
背面图案：熊猫饮水图

编码：2013-0207-Au-5oz#
背面图案：熊猫饮水图

共同正面
正面图案：北京天坛祈年殿

编码：2013-0209-Ag-5oz#
背面图案：熊猫饮水图

编码：2013-0208-Ag-1kg#
背面图案：熊猫饮水图

正面图案：北京天坛祈年殿

编码：2013-0210-Ag-1oz#
背面图案：熊猫饮水图

上海浦东发展银行成立20周年熊猫加字金银纪念币

The 20th Anniversary of Shanghai Pudong Development Bank Panda Gold and Silver Commemorative Coins

正面图案：北京天坛祈年殿

编码：2013-0301-Au-1/4oz#
背面图案：熊猫饮水图

正面图案：北京天坛祈年殿

编码：2013-0302-Ag-1oz#
背面图案：熊猫饮水图

本套币正面图稿设计者：孙奇龄
正面浮雕制作者：岳俊峰
背面图稿设计者：程　超
背面浮雕制作者：余　敏

金币1枚　银币1枚　1 Gold Coin　1 Silver Coin

编码	材质	质量	重量(盎司)	直径(毫米)	面额(元)	成色(%)	最大发行量(枚)	铸造单位
2013-0301-Au-1/4oz#	金币	普制	1/4	22	100	99.9	30000	深圳
2013-0302-Ag-1oz#	银币	普制	1	40	10	99.9	80000	深圳

中国光大集团成立30周年熊猫加字金银纪念币

The 30th Anniversary of China Everbright Group Panda Gold and Silver Commemorative Coins

正面图案：
北京天坛祈年殿

编码：2013-0801-Au-1/4oz#
背面图案：熊猫饮水图

正面图案：北京天坛祈年殿

编码：2013-0802-Ag-1oz#
背面图案：熊猫饮水图

本套币正面图稿设计者：孙奇龄
正面浮雕制作者：岳俊峰
背面图稿设计者：程　超
背面浮雕制作者：余　敏

金币1枚 银币1枚　1 Gold Coin 1 Silver Coin

编码	材质	质量	重量(盎司)	直径(毫米)	面额(元)	成色(%)	最大发行量(枚)	铸造单位
2013-0801-Au-1/4oz#	金币	普制	1/4	22	100	99.9	10000	深圳
2013-0802-Ag-1oz#	银币	普制	1	40	10	99.9	30000	深圳

中国—东盟博览会10周年熊猫加字金银纪念币

The 10th Anniversary of China-ASEAN Exposition Panda Gold and Silver Commemorative Coins

正面图案：
北京天坛祈年殿

编码：2013-0901-Au-1/4oz#
背面图案：熊猫饮水图

正面图案：北京天坛祈年殿

编码：2013-0902-Ag-1oz#
背面图案：熊猫饮水图

本套币正面图稿设计者：孙奇龄
正面浮雕制作者：岳俊峰
背面图稿设计者：程　超
背面浮雕制作者：余　敏

金币1枚 银币1枚　1 Gold Coin 1 Silver Coin

编码	材质	质量	重量(盎司)	直泾(毫米)	面额(元)	成色(%)	最大发行量(枚)	铸造单位
2013-0901-Au-1/4oz#	金币	普制	1/4	22	100	99.9	15000	深圳
2013-0902-Ag-1oz#	银币	普制	1	40	10	99.9	30000	深圳

中国—东盟博览会10周年熊猫加字金银纪念币

The 10th Anniversary of China-ASEAN Exposition Panda Gold and Silver Commemorative Coins

正面图案：中华人民共和国国徽及连年有余吉祥纹饰
设计者：张文静
浮雕制作者：集体

癸巳

100000元

2013中国癸巳（蛇）年金银纪念币

2013 Chinese Gui Si Year (Year of the Snake) Gold and Silver Commemorative Coins

编码：2013-0101-Au-10kg
背面图案：写实蛇图形及装饰蛇纹样
设计者：朱熙华　何云　何忠
浮雕制作者：邓姗姗

正面图案：中华人民共和国国徽及连年有余吉祥纹饰
设计者：张文静　浮雕制作者：集体

编码：2013-0102-Au-1kg
背面图案：写实蛇图形及装饰蛇纹样
设计者：朱熙华　何忠　何云　浮雕制作者：邓姗姗

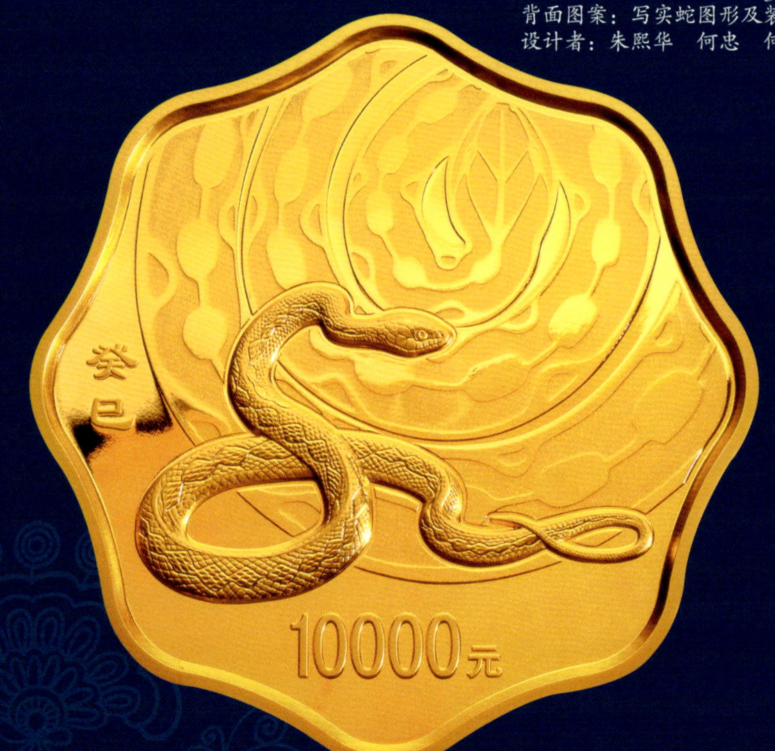

2013中国癸巳（蛇）年金银纪念币

2013 Chinese Gui Si Year (Year of the Snake) Gold and Silver Commemorative Coins

正面图案：中华人民共和国国徽及连年有余吉祥纹饰
设计者：张文静
浮雕制作者：集体

编码：2013-0103-Au-5oz
背面图案：中国民间传统装饰蛇图形及吉祥纹饰
设计者：张文静　何忠　何云
浮雕制作者：宋飞

金币8枚　银币7枚　8 Gold Coins　7 Silver Coins

编码	材质	质量	重量(盎司)	形制尺寸(毫米)	面额(元)	成色(%)	最大发行量(枚)	铸造单位
2013-0101-Au-10kg	金币	精制	10公斤	圆形直径180	100000	99.9	18	上海
2013-0102-Au-1kg	金币	精制	1公斤	梅花形外接圆直径100	10000	99.9	118	深圳
2013-0103-Au-5oz	彩色金币	精制	5	圆形直径60	2000	99.9	3000	深圳
2013-0104-Au-5oz	金币	精制	5	长方形64×40	2000	99.9	2000	沈阳
2013-0105-Au-1/2oz	金币	精制	1/2	梅花形外接圆直径27	200	99.9	8000	上海
2013-0106-Au-1/3oz	金币	精制	1/3	扇形外圆半径51，内圆半径36，圆心角30度	150	99.9	30000	深圳
2013-0107-Au-1/10oz	彩色金币	精制	1/10	圆形直径18	50	99.9	120000	上海
2013-0108-Au-1/10oz	金币	精制	1/10	圆形直径18	50	99.9	120000	沈阳
2013-0109-Ag-1kg	银币	精制	1公斤	圆形直径100	300	99.9	3800	深圳
2013-0110-Ag-5oz	彩色银币	精制	5	圆形直径70	50	99.9	30000	上海
2013-0111-Ag-5oz	银币	精制	5	长方形80×50	50	99.9	20000	深圳
2013-0112-Ag-1oz	彩色银币	精制	1	圆形直径40	10	99.9	220000	沈阳
2013-0113-Ag-1oz	银币	精制	1	梅花形外接圆直径40	10	99.9	60000	上海
2013-0114-Ag-1oz	银币	精制	1	扇形外圆半径85，内圆半径60，圆心角30度	10	99.9	80000	深圳
2013-0115-Ag-1oz	银币	精制	1	圆形直径40	10	99.9	200000	上海

正面图案：中华人民共和国国徽及连年有余吉祥纹饰
设计者：张文静
浮雕制作者：集体

编码：2013-0104-Au-5oz
背面图案：写实蛇图形及装饰蛇纹样
设计者：朱熙华　何忠　何云
浮雕制作者：邓姗姗

2013中国癸巳（蛇）年金银纪念币

2013 Chinese Gui Si Year (Year of the Snake) Gold and Silver Commemorative Coins

正面图案：中华人民共和国国徽及连年有余吉祥纹饰
设计者：张文静
浮雕制作者：集体

编码：2013-0105-Au-1/2oz
背面图案：写实蛇图形及装饰蛇纹样
设计者：朱熙华　何忠　何云
浮雕制作者：邓姗姗

正面图案：中华人民共和国国徽及连年有余吉祥纹饰
设计者：张文静
浮雕制作者：集体

编码：2013-0106-Au-1/3oz
背面图案：写实蛇图形及装饰蛇纹样
设计者：朱熙华　何忠　何云
浮雕制作者：邓姗姗

共同正面
正面图案：中华人民共和国国徽及连年有余吉祥纹饰
设计者：张文静
浮雕制作者：集体

编码：2013-0107-Au-1/10oz
背面图案：中国民间传统装饰蛇图形及吉祥纹饰
设计者：张文静　何忠　何云
浮雕制作者：张春晔

编码：2013-0108-Au-1/10oz
背面图案：写实蛇图形及装饰蛇纹样
设计者：朱熙华　何忠　何云
浮雕制作者：邓姗姗

正面图案：中华人民共和国国徽及连年有余吉祥纹饰
设计者：张文静
浮雕制作者：集体

2013中国癸巳（蛇）年金银纪念币

2013 Chinese Gui Si Year (Year of the Snake) Gold and Silver Commemorative Coins

编码：2013-0109-Ag-1kg
背面图案：写实蛇图形及装饰蛇纹样
设计者：朱熙华　何忠　何云
浮雕制作者：邓姗姗

正面图案：中华人民共和国国徽及连年有余吉祥纹饰
设计者：张文静
浮雕制作者：集体

编码：2013-0110-Ag-5oz
背面图案：中国民间传统装饰蛇图形及吉祥纹饰
设计者：张文静　何忠　何云
浮雕制作者：张春晔

正面图案：中华人民共和国国徽及连年有余吉祥纹饰
设计者：张文静
浮雕制作者：集体

编码：2013-0111-Ag-5oz
背面图案：写实蛇图形及装饰蛇纹样
设计者：朱熙华　何忠　何云
浮雕制作者：邓姗姗

正面图案：中华人民共和国国徽
及连年有余吉祥纹饰
设计者：张文静
浮雕制作者：集体

编码：2013-0112-Ag-1oz
背面图案：中国民间传统装饰蛇图形及吉祥纹饰
设计者：张文静　何忠　何云
浮雕制作者：常欢　富丽莉

正面图案：中华人民共和国国徽
及连年有余吉祥纹饰
设计者：张文静
浮雕制作者：集体

编码：2013-0113-Ag-1oz
背面图案：写实蛇图形及装饰蛇纹样
设计者：朱熙华　何忠　何云
浮雕制作者：邓姗姗

2013中国癸巳（蛇）年金银纪念币

2013 Chinese Gui Si Year (Year of the Snake) Gold and Silver Commemorative Coins

正面图案：中华人民共和国国徽
及连年有余吉祥纹饰
设计者：张文静
浮雕制作者：集体

编码：2013-0114-Ag-1oz
背面图案：写实蛇图形及装饰蛇纹样
设计者：朱熙华　何忠　何云
浮雕制作者：邓姗姗

正面图案：中华人民共和国国徽
及连年有余吉祥纹饰
设计者：张文静
浮雕制作者：集体

编码：2013-0115-Ag-1oz
背面图案：写实蛇图形及装饰蛇纹样
设计者：朱熙华　何忠　何云
浮雕制作者：邓姗姗

北斗卫星导航系统开通运行金银纪念币

Gold and Silver Commemorative Coins for the Start of the Operation of Compass Navigation Satellite System

正面图案：中华人民共和国国徽
设计者：中国金币总公司提供　浮雕制作者：集体

编码：2013-0401-Au-1/3oz
背面图案：眼睛造型及地球、卫星、北斗七星、二进制码
设计者：王玲、程超　浮雕制作者：胥喻婷

正面图案：中华人民共和国国徽
设计者：中国金币总公司提供　浮雕制作者：集体

编码：2013-0402-Ag-1oz
背面图案：指北针造型及卫星、北斗七星、二进制码
设计者：王玲、程超　浮雕制作者：陈彦文

金币1枚　银币1枚　1 Gold Coin　1 Silver Coin

编码	材质	质量	重量(盎司)	直径(毫米)	面额(元)	成色(%)	最大发行量(枚)	铸造单位
2013-0401-Au-1/3oz	金币	精制	1/3	23	150	99.9	30000	上海
2013-0402-Ag-1oz	银币	精制	1	40	10	99.9	60000	上海

北斗卫星导航系统开通运行金银纪念币

Gold and Silver Commemorative Coins for the Start of the Operation of Compass Navigation Satellite System

正面图案：中华人民共和国国徽
设计者：中国金币总公司提供
浮雕制作者：集体

编码：2013-0501-Au-1kg
背面图案：南海观音造像、“海天佛国图”景观及海水纹饰
设计者：邱燕新
浮雕制作者：张磊

中国佛教圣地（普陀山）金银纪念币

Chinese Sacred Buddhist Mountain (Mount Putuo) Gold and Silver Commemorative Coins

金币3枚 银币2枚 3 Gold Coins 2 Silver Coins

编码	材质	质量	重量(盎司)	直径(毫米)	面额(元)	成色(%)	最大发行量(枚)	铸造单位
2013-0501-Au-1kg	金币	精制	1公斤	90	10000	99.9	300	深圳
2013-0502-Au-5oz	金币	精制	5	60	2000	99.9	3000	深圳
2013-0503-Au-1/4oz	金币	精制	1/4	22	100	99.9	60000	深圳
2013-0504-Ag-1kg	银币	精制	1公斤	100	300	99.9	10000	深圳
2013-0505-Ag-2oz	银币	精制	2	40	20	99.9	100000	深圳

共同正面
正面图案：中华人民共和国国徽
设计者：中国金币总公司提供
浮雕制作者：集体

编码：2013-0502-Au-5oz
背面图案：毗卢观音造像及海水纹饰
设计者：邱燕新
浮雕制作者：张江

编码：2013-0503-Au-1/4oz
背面图案：杨枝观音造像及祥云、海水纹饰
设计者：王安云
浮雕制作者：禹飞

正面图案：中华人民共和国国徽
设计者：中国金币总公司提供
浮雕制作者：集体

编码：2013-0505-Ag-2oz
背面图案：普济寺建筑群及海水纹饰
设计者：姚有均
浮雕制作者：钟承辛

正面图案：中华人民共和国国徽
设计者：中国金币总公司提供
浮雕制作者：集体

中国佛教圣地（普陀山）金银纪念币

Chinese Sacred Buddhist Mountain (Mount Putuo) Gold and Silver Commemorative Coins

编码：2013-0504-Ag-1kg
背面图案："海天佛国图"景观及海水纹饰
设计者：王云野
浮雕制作者：李震凯

正面图案：中华人民共和国国徽
设计者：中国金币总公司提供
浮雕制作者：集体

编码：2013-0604-Ag-5oz
背面图案：商代司母辛觥
设计者：邱燕新
浮雕制作者：蔡冥昱

正面图案：中华人民共和国国徽
设计者：中国金币总公司提供
浮雕制作者：集体

编码：2013-0605-Ag-1oz
背面图案：商代妇好方斝
设计者：邱燕新
浮雕制作者：费庆东

世界遗产
WORLD HERITAGE · PATRIMOINE MONDIAL

正面图案：中华人民共和国国徽
设计者：中国金币总公司提供
浮雕制作者：集体

世界遗产——黄山金银纪念币

World Heritage—Huangshan Mountain Gold and Silver Commemorative Coins

编码：2013-0701-Au-1kg
背面图案："迎客松"景观
设计者：周剑　夏子庆
浮雕制作者：田晓斌

正面图案：中华人民共和国国徽
设计者：中国金币总公司提供
浮雕制作者：集体

编码：2013-0702-Au-5oz
背面图案："梦笔生花"景观
设计者：姚有均
浮雕制作者：韩晓生

正面图案：中华人民共和国国徽
设计者：中国金币总公司提供
浮雕制作者：集体

编码：2013-0703-Au-1/4oz
背面图案："迎客松"景观
设计者：朱熙华
浮雕制作者：姜茜茜

金币3枚 银币5枚 3 Gold Coins 5 Silver Coins

编码	材质	质量	重量(盎司)	直径(毫米)	面额(元)	成色(%)	最大发行量(枚)	铸造单位
2013-0701-Au-1kg	金币	精制	1公斤	90	10000	99.9	200	深圳
2013-0702-Au-5oz	金币	精制	5	60	2000	99.9	1000	沈阳
2013-0703-Au-1/4oz	金币	精制	1/4	22	100	99.9	30000	深圳
2013-0704-Ag-1kg	银币	精制	1公斤	100	300	99.9	5000	深圳
2013-0705-Ag-1oz	银币	精制	1	40	10	99.9	50000	沈阳
2013-0706-Ag-1oz	银币	精制	1	40	10	99.9	50000	上海
2013-0707-Ag-1oz	银币	精制	1	40	10	99.9	50000	深圳
2013-0708-Ag-1oz	银币	精制	1	40	10	99.9	50000	沈阳

正面图案：中华人民共和国国徽
设计者：中国金币总公司提供
浮雕制作者：集体

世界遗产——黄山金银纪念币

World Heritage—Huangshan Mountain Gold and Silver Commemorative Coins

编码：2013-0704-Ag-1kg
背面图案：“玉屏胜景”景观
设计者：周剑　夏子庆
浮雕制作者：张磊

共同正面
正面图案：中华人民共和国国徽
设计者：中国金币总公司提供
浮雕制作者：集体

编码：2013-0705-Ag-1oz
背面图案："猴子观海"景观
设计者：姚有均
浮雕制作者：侯继强

编码：2013-0706-Ag-1oz
背面图案："飞来石"景观
设计者：周剑　夏子庆
浮雕制作者：张春晔

编码：2013-0707-Ag-1oz
背面图案："人字瀑"景观
设计者：王云野
浮雕制作者：魏雪飞

编码：2013-0708-Ag-1oz
背面图案："玉屏楼"景观
设计者：王云野
浮雕制作者：王云野

世界遗产——黄山金银纪念币

World Heritage—Huangshan Mountain Gold and Silver Commemorative Coins

2013北京国际钱币博览会银质纪念币

The Commemorative Silver Coin for Beijing International Coin Exposition 2013

编码：2013-1001-Ag-1oz

背面图案：中国明代钱币与奥地利哈布斯堡王朝钱币

设计者：齐云兰

浮雕制作者：张磊

正面图案：象征钱币、地球的点线图案与2013北京国际钱币博览会会标

设计者：朱熙华

浮雕制作者：禹飞

银币1枚　1 Silver Coin

编码	材质	质量	重量(盎司)	直径(毫米)	面额(元)	成色(%)	最大发行量(枚)	铸造单位
2013-1001-Ag-1oz	银币	精制	1	40	10	99.9	30000	深圳

2014

2014版熊猫金银纪念币

2014 Chinese Panda Gold and Silver Commemorative Coins

2014青岛世界园艺博览会熊猫加字金银纪念币

The International Horticultural Exposition 2014 Qingdao Panda Gold and Silver Commemorative Coins

中国建设银行成立60周年熊猫加字金银纪念币

The 60th Anniversary of China Construction Bank Panda Gold and Silver Commemorative Coins

中国农业发展银行成立20周年熊猫加字银质纪念币

The 20th Anniversary of the Agricultural Development Bank of China Panda Commemorative Silver Coin

2014中国甲午（马）年金银纪念币

2014 Chinese Jia Wu Year (Year of the Horse) Gold and Silver Commemorative Coins

中国探月首次落月成功金银纪念币

China Lunar Exploration Program's First Successful Moon Landing Gold and Silver Commemorative Coins

第二届夏季青年奥林匹克运动会金银纪念币

The Gold and Silver Commemorative Coins for

the 2nd Summer Youth Olympic Games, Nanjing 2014

中国—法国建交50周年金银纪念币

The 50th Anniversary of Diplomatic Relations Between China and France Gold and Silver Commemorative Coins

中国佛教圣地（峨眉山）金银纪念币

Chinese Sacred Buddhist Mountain (Mount Emei) Gold and Silver Commemorative Coins

世界遗产——杭州西湖文化景观金银纪念币

World Heritage -- West Lake Cultural Landscape of Hangzhou Gold and Silver Commemorative Coins

新疆生产建设兵团成立60周年金银纪念币

The 60th Anniversary of Xinjiang Production and Construction Corps Gold and Silver Commemorative Coins

中国青铜器金银纪念币(第3组）

The Chinese Bronze Ware Gold and Silver Commemorative Coins (3rd Issue)

2014北京国际钱币博览会银质纪念币

The Commemorative Silver Coin for Beijing International Coin Exposition 2014

2014版熊猫金银纪念币

2014 Chinese Panda Gold and Silver Commemorative Coins

2014青岛世界园艺博览会熊猫加字金银纪念币

The International Horticultural Exposition 2014 Qingdao Panda Gold and Silver Commemorative Coins

中国建设银行成立60周年熊猫加字金银纪念币

The 60th Anniversary of China Construction Bank Panda Gold and Silver Commemorative Coins

中国农业发展银行成立20周年熊猫加字银质纪念币

The 20th Anniversary of the Agricultural Development Bank of China Panda Commemorative Silver Coin

2014中国甲午（马）年金银纪念币

2014 Chinese Jia Wu Year (Year of the Horse) Gold and Silver Commemorative Coins

中国探月首次落月成功金银纪念币

China Lunar Exploration Program's First Successful Moon Landing Gold and Silver Commemorative Coins

第二届夏季青年奥林匹克运动会金银纪念币

The Gold and Silver Commemorative Coins for

the 2nd Summer Youth Olympic Games, Nanjing 2014

中国—法国建交50周年金银纪念币

The 50th Anniversary of Diplomatic Relations Between China and France Gold and Silver Commemorative Coins

中国佛教圣地（峨眉山）金银纪念币

Chinese Sacred Buddhist Mountain (Mount Emei) Gold and Silver Commemorative Coins

世界遗产——杭州西湖文化景观金银纪念币

World Heritage—West Lake Cultural Landscape of Hangzhou Gold and Silver Commemorative Coins

新疆生产建设兵团成立60周年金银纪念币

The 60th Anniversary of Xinjiang Production and Construction Corps Gold and Silver Commemorative Coins

中国青铜器金银纪念币（第3组）

The Chinese Bronze Ware Gold and Silver Commemorative Coins (3rd Issue)

2014北京国际钱币博览会银质纪念币

The Commemorative Silver Coin for Beijing International Coin Exposition 2014

2014版熊猫金银纪念币

2014 Chinese Panda Gold and Silver Commemorative Coins

共同正面
正面图案：北京天坛祈年殿

编码：2014-0101-Au-1oz#
背面图案：熊猫嬉戏图

编码：2014-0102-Au-1/2oz#
背面图案：熊猫嬉戏图

编码：2014-0103-Au-1/4oz#
背面图案：熊猫嬉戏图

编码：2014-0104-Au-1/10oz#
背面图案：熊猫嬉戏图

编码：2014-0105-Au-1/20oz#
背面图案：熊猫嬉戏图

本套币正面图稿设计者：孙奇龄
正面浮雕制作者：岳俊峰
背面图稿设计者：赵　樯
背面浮雕制作者：张　磊

金币7枚　银币3枚　7 Gold Coins 3 Silver Coins

编码	材质	质量	重量(盎司)	直径(毫米)	面额(元)	成色(%)	最大发行量(枚)	铸造单位
2014-0101-Au-1oz#	金币	普制	1	32	500	99.9	1000000	上海、沈阳、深圳
2014-0102-Au-1/2oz#	金币	普制	1/2	27	200	99.9	600000	上海、沈阳、深圳
2014-0103-Au-1/4oz#	金币	普制	1/4	22	100	99.9	600000	上海、沈阳、深圳
2014-0104-Au-1/10oz#	金币	普制	1/10	18	50	99.9	800000	上海、沈阳、深圳
2014-0105-Au-1/20oz#	金币	普制	1/20	14	20	99.9	800000	上海、沈阳、深圳
2014-0106-Au-1kg#	金币	精制	1公斤	90	10000	99.9	500	沈阳
2014-0107-Au-5oz#	金币	精制	5	60	2000	99.9	5000	沈阳
2014-0108-Ag-1kg#	银币	精制	1公斤	100	300	99.9	20000	沈阳
2014-0109-Ag-5oz#	银币	精制	5	70	50	99.9	50000	沈阳
2014-0110-Ag-1oz#	银币	普制	1	40	10	99.9	8000000	上海、沈阳、深圳

共同正面
正面图案：北京天坛祈年殿

编码：2014-0106-Au-1kg#
背面图案：熊猫嬉戏图

编码：2014-0107-Au-5oz#
背面图案：熊猫嬉戏图

共同正面
正面图案：北京天坛祈年殿

编码：2014-0108-Ag-1kg#
背面图案：熊猫嬉戏图

2014版熊猫金银纪念币

2014 Chinese Panda Gold and Silver Commemorative Coins

编码：2014-0109-Ag-5oz#
背面图案：熊猫嬉戏图

正面图案：北京天坛祈年殿

编码：2014-0110-Ag-1oz#
背面图案：熊猫嬉戏图

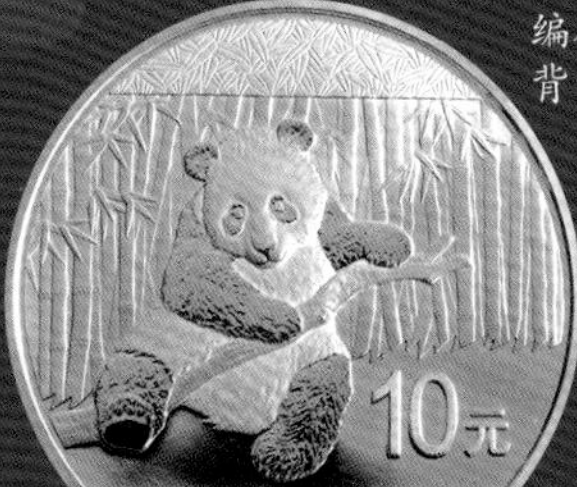

2014青岛世界园艺博览会熊猫加字金银纪念币

The International Horticultural Exposition 2014 Qingdao Panda Gold and Silver Commemorative Coins

正面图案：北京天坛祈年殿

编码：2014-0701-Au-1/4oz#
背面图案：熊猫嬉戏图

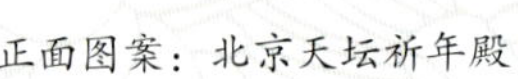
正面图案：北京天坛祈年殿

编码：2014-0702-Ag-1oz#
背面图案：熊猫嬉戏图

本套币正面图稿设计者：孙奇龄
正面浮雕制作者：岳俊峰
背面图稿设计者：赵 樯
背面浮雕制作者：张 磊

金币1枚 银币1枚 1 Gold Coin 1 Silver Coin

编码	材质	质量	重量(盎司)	直径(毫米)	面额(元)	成色(%)	最大发行量(枚)	铸造单位
2014-0701-Au-1/4oz#	金币	普制	1/4	22	100	99.9	8000	深圳
2014-0702-Ag-1oz#	银币	普制	1	40	10	99.9	40000	深圳

2014青岛世界园艺博览会熊猫加字金银纪念币

The International Horticultural Exposition 2014 Qingdao Panda Gold and Silver Commemorative Coins

中国建设银行成立60周年熊猫加字金银纪念币

The 60th Anniversary of China Construction Bank Panda Gold and Silver Commemorative Coins

共同正面
正面图案：北京天坛祈年殿

编码：2014-1001-Au-1oz#
背面图案：熊猫嬉戏图

编码：2014-1002-Au-1/4oz#
背面图案：熊猫嬉戏图

正面图案：北京天坛祈年殿

编码：2014-1003-Ag-1oz#
背面图案：熊猫嬉戏图

本套币正面图稿设计者：孙奇龄
正面浮雕制作者：岳俊峰
背面图稿设计者：赵　樯
背面浮雕制作者：张　磊

金币2枚 银币1枚　2 Gold Coins 1 Silver Coin

编码	材质	质量	重量(盎司)	直径(毫米)	面额(元)	成色(%)	最大发行量(枚)	铸造单位
2014-1001-Au-1oz#	金币	普制	1	32	500	99.9	22000	深圳
2014-1002-Au-1/4oz#	金币	普制	1/4	22	100	99.9	75000	深圳
2014-1003-Ag-1oz#	银币	普制	1	40	10	99.9	420000	深圳

中国农业发展银行成立20周年熊猫加字银质纪念币

The 20th Anniversary of the Agricultural Development Bank of China Panda Commemorative Silver Coin

编码：2014-1301-Ag-1oz#
背面图案：熊猫嬉戏图

正面图案：北京天坛祈年殿

本套币正面图稿设计者：孙奇龄
正面浮雕制作者：岳俊峰
背面图稿设计者：赵 樯
背面浮雕制作者：张 磊

银币1枚 1 Silver Coin

编码	材质	质量	重量(盎司)	直径(毫米)	面额(元)	成色(%)	最大发行量(枚)	铸造单位
2014-1301-Ag-1oz#	银币	普制	1	40	10	99.9	85000	深圳

正面图案：中华人民共和国国徽及连年有余吉祥纹饰
设计者：张文静
浮雕制作者：集体

2014中国甲午（马）年金银纪念币

2014 Chinese Jia Wu Year (Year of the Horse) Gold and Silver Commemorative Coins

编码：2014-0201-Au-10kg
背面图案：奔马图及装饰马首
设计者：朱熙华
浮雕制作者：张磊

韓幹畫照夜白

正面图案：中华人民共和国国徽及连年有余吉祥纹饰
设计者：张文静
浮雕制作者：集体

2014中国甲午（马）年金银纪念币

2014 Chinese Jia Wu Year (Year of the Horse) Gold and Silver Commemorative Coins

编码：2014-0202-Au-2kg
背面图案：奔马图及装饰马首
设计者：朱熙华
浮雕制作者：张磊

正面图案：中华人民共和国国徽及连年有余吉祥纹饰
设计者：张文静
浮雕制作者：集体

编码：2014-0203-Au-1kg
背面图案：奔马图及装饰马首
设计者：朱熙华
浮雕制作者：张磊

正面图案：中华人民共和国国徽及连年有余吉祥纹饰
设计者：张文静
浮雕制作者：集体

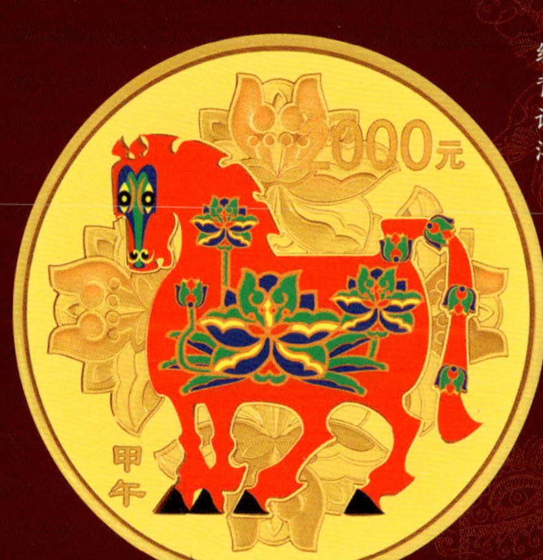

编码：2014-0204-Au-5oz
背面图案：中国民间传统装饰马图形及吉祥纹饰
设计者：张文静　何忠　何洁
浮雕制作者：常欢　富丽莉

2014中国甲午（马）年金银纪念币

2014 Chinese Jia Wu Year (Year of the Horse) Gold and Silver Commemorative Coins

金币9枚　银币7枚　9 Gold Coins 7 Silver Coins

编码	材质	质量	重量(盎司)	形制尺寸(毫米)	面额(元)	成色(%)	最大发行量(枚)	铸造单位
2014-0201-Au-10kg	金币	精制	10公斤	圆形直径180	100000	99.9	18	深圳
2014-0202-Au-2kg	金币	精制	2公斤	圆形直径110	20000	99.9	100	深圳
2014-0203-Au-1kg	金币	精制	1公斤	梅花形外接圆直径100	10000	99.9	118	深圳
2014-0204-Au-5oz	彩色金币	精制	5	圆形直径60	2000	99.9	3000	沈阳
2014-0205-Au-5oz	金币	精制	5	长方形64×40	2000	99.9	2000	沈阳
2014-0206-Au-1/2oz	金币	精制	1/2	梅花形外接圆直径27	200	99.9	8000	深圳
2014-0207-Au-1/3oz	金币	精制	1/3	扇形外圆半径51，内圆半径36，圆心角30度	150	99.9	30000	深圳
2014-0208-Au-1/10oz	彩色金币	精制	1/10	圆形直径18	50	99.9	120000	上海
2014-0209-Au-1/10oz	金币	精制	1/10	圆形直径18	50	99.9	120000	深圳
2014-0210-Ag-1kg	银币	精制	1公斤	圆形直径100	300	99.9	10000	深圳
2014-0211-Ag-5oz	彩色银币	精制	5	圆形直径70	50	99.9	30000	上海
2014-0212-Ag-5oz	银币	精制	5	长方形80×50	50	99.9	20000	上海
2014-0213-Ag-1oz	彩色银币	精制	1	圆形直径40	10	99.9	220000	沈阳
2014-0214-Ag-1oz	银币	精制	1	梅花形外接圆直径40	10	99.9	60000	深圳
2014-0215-Ag-1oz	银币	精制	1	扇形外圆半径85，内圆半径60，圆心角30度	10	99.9	80000	深圳
2014-0216-Ag-1oz	银币	精制	1	圆形直径 40	10	99.9	200000	深圳

正面图案：中华人民共和国国徽及连年有余吉祥纹饰
设计者：张文静
浮雕制作者：集体

编码：2014-0205-Au-5oz
背面图案：奔马图及装饰马首
设计者：朱熙华
浮雕制作者：张磊 廖博

正面图案：中华人民共和国国徽及连年有余吉祥纹饰
设计者：张文静
浮雕制作者：集体

编码：2014-0206-Au-1/2oz
背面图案：奔马图及装饰马首
设计者：朱熙华
浮雕制作者：张磊

编码：2014-0207-Au-1/3oz
背面图案：奔马图及装饰马首
设计者：朱熙华
浮雕制作者：张磊

正面图案：中华人民共和国国徽及连年有余吉祥纹饰
设计者：张文静
浮雕制作者：集体

2014中国甲午（马）年金银纪念币

2014 Chinese Jia Wu Year (Year of the Horse) Gold and Silver Commemorative Coins

共同正面

正面图案：中华人民共和国国徽及连年有余

吉祥纹饰

设计者：张文静

浮雕制作者：集体

编码：2014-0208-Au-1/10oz

背面图案：中国民间传统装饰马图形及吉祥纹饰

设计者：张文静　何忠　何云

浮雕制作者：张春晔

编码：2014-0209-Au-1/10oz

背面图案：奔马图及装饰马首

设计者：朱熙华

浮雕制作者：张磊

正面图案：中华人民共和国国徽及连年有余吉祥纹饰
设计者：张文静
浮雕制作者：集体

编码：2014-0210-Ag-1kg
背面图案：奔马图及装饰马首
设计者：朱熙华
浮雕制作者：张磊

2014中国甲午（马）年金银纪念币

2014 Chinese Jia Wu Year (Year of the Horse) Gold and Silver Commemorative Coins

正面图案：中华人民共和国国徽及连年有余吉祥纹饰
设计者：张文静
浮雕制作者：集体

编码：2014-0211-Ag-5oz
背面图案：中国民间传统装饰马图形及吉祥纹饰
设计者：张文静 何忠 何云
浮雕制作者：张春晔

正面图案：中华人民共和国国徽及连年有余吉祥纹饰
设计者：张文静
浮雕制作者：集体

编码：2014-0212-Ag-5oz
背面图案：奔马图及装饰马首
设计者：朱熙华
浮雕制作者：张磊

正面图案：中华人民共和国国徽
及连年有余吉祥纹饰
设计者：张文静
浮雕制作者：集体

编码：2014-0213-Ag-1oz
背面图案：中国民间传统装饰马图形及吉祥纹饰
设计者：张文静　何忠　何云
浮雕制作者：常欢　富丽莉

正面图案：中华人民共和国国徽及连年有余吉祥纹饰
设计者：张文静
浮雕制作者：集体

编码：2014-0214-Ag-1oz
背面图案：奔马图及装饰马首
设计者：朱熙华
浮雕制作者：张磊

正面图案：中华人民共和国国徽
及连年有余吉祥纹饰
设计者：张文静
浮雕制作者：集体

编码：2014-0215-Ag-1oz
背面图案：奔马图及装饰马首
设计者：朱熙华
浮雕制作者：张磊

正面图案：中华人民共和国国徽
及连年有余吉祥纹饰
设计者：张文静
浮雕制作者：集体

编码：2014-0216-Ag-1oz
背面图案：奔马图及装饰马首
设计者：朱熙华
浮雕制作者：张磊

2014中国甲午（马）年金银纪念币

2014 Chinese Jia Wu Year (Year of the Horse) Gold and Silver Commemorative Coins

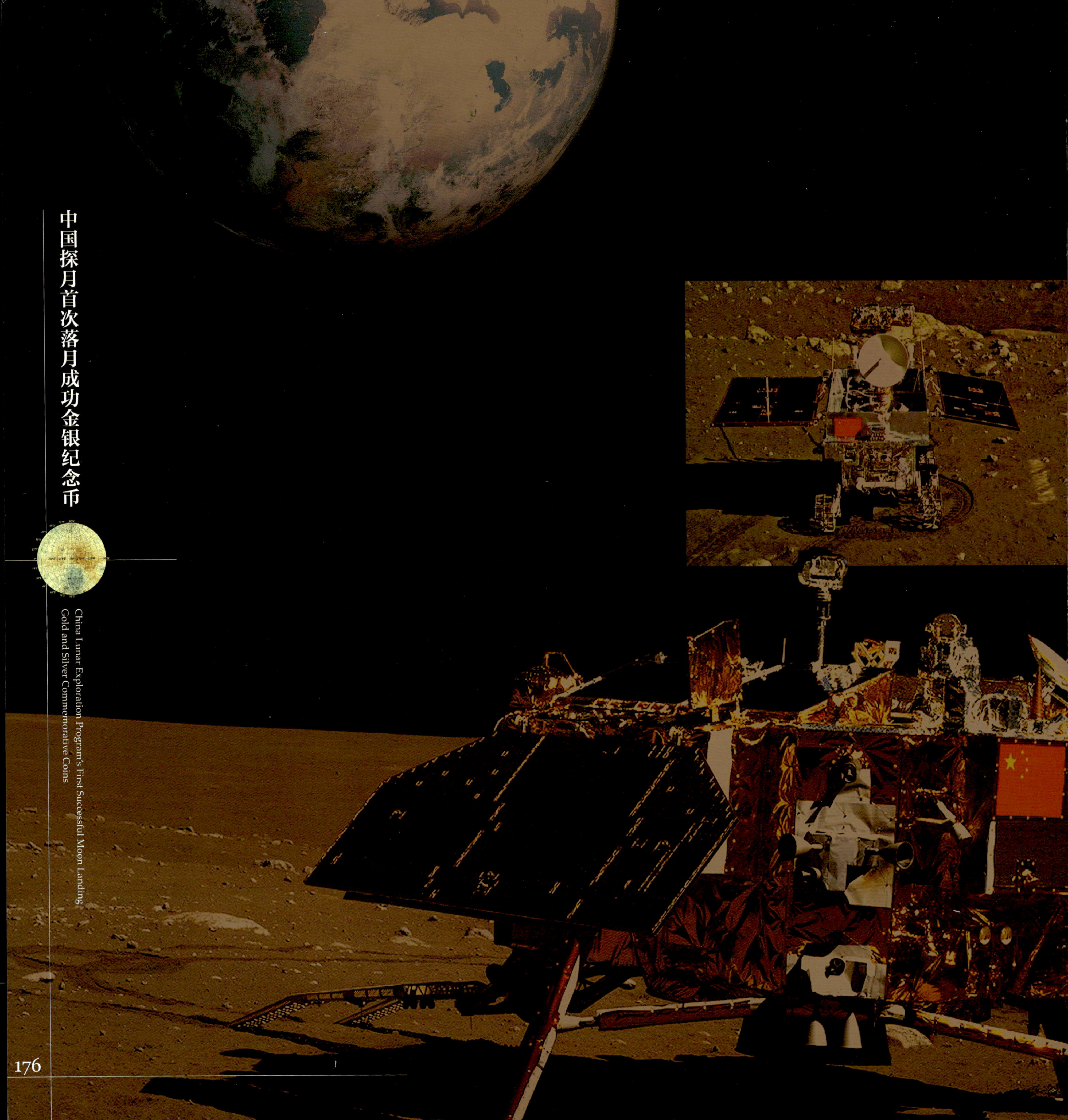

中国探月首次落月成功金银纪念币

China Lunar Exploration Program's First Successful Moon Landing Gold and Silver Commemorative Coins

中国探月首次落月成功金银纪念币

China Lunar Exploration Program's First Successful Moon Landing Gold and Silver Commemorative Coins

正面图案：中华人民共和国国徽
设计者：中国金币总公司提供
浮雕制作者：集体

编码：2014-0301-Au-1/4oz
背面图案："月球车"月面巡视勘测
设计者：邱燕新　周剑
浮雕制作者：费庆东　邓姗姗

正面图案：中华人民共和国国徽
设计者：中国金币总公司提供
浮雕制作者：集体

编码：2014-0302-Ag-1oz
背面图案："着陆器"与"月球车"月面互拍
设计者：邓姗姗　钟承辛
浮雕制作者：钟承辛

金币1枚　银币1枚　1 Gold Coin 1 Silver Coin

编码	材质	质量	重量(盎司)	直径(毫米)	面额(元)	成色(%)	最大发行量(枚)	铸造单位
2014-0301-Au-1/4oz	金币	精制	1/4	22	100	99.9	10000	深圳
2014-0302-Ag-1oz	银币	精制	1	40	10	99.9	20000	深圳

第二届夏季青年奥林匹克运动会金银纪念币

The Gold and Silver Commemorative Coins for the 2nd Summer Youth Olympic Games, Nanjing 2014

正面图案：中华人民共和国国徽
设计者：中国金币总公司提供
浮雕制作者：集体

编码：2014-0401-Au-1/4oz
背面图案：标准吉祥物及装饰跑道
设计者：董慧珍
浮雕制作者：田晓斌

共同正面
正面图案：中华人民共和国国徽
设计者：中国金币总公司提供
浮雕制作者：集体

编码：2014-0402-Ag-5oz
背面图案：青奥会会徽及南京城门、云锦纹饰
设计者：张琛琛
浮雕制作者：金雅轩

编码：2014-0403-Ag-1/2oz
背面图案：高尔夫球运动吉祥物及装饰梅花
设计者：陈彦文
浮雕制作者：陈彦文

编码：2014-0404-Ag-1/2oz
背面图案：橄榄球运动吉祥物及装饰梅花
设计者：陈彦文
浮雕制作者：姜茜茜

金币1枚 银币3枚 1 Gold Coin 3 Silver Coins

编码	材质	质量	重量(盎司)	直径(毫米)	面额(元)	成色(%)	最大发行量(枚)	铸造单位
2014-0401-Au-1/4oz	金币	精制	1/4	22	100	99.9	10000	深圳
2014-0402-Ag-5oz	银币	精制	5	70	50	99.9	2000	沈阳
2014-0403-Ag-1/2oz	银币	精制	1/2	33	5	99.9	20000	上海
2014-0404-Ag-1oz	银币	精制	1/2	33	5	99.9	20000	深圳

中国—法国建交50周年金银纪念币

50周年

The 50th Anniversary of Diplomatic Relations Between China and France Gold and Silver Commemorative Coins

正面图案：中华人民共和国国徽
设计者：中国金币总公司提供
浮雕制作者：集体

编码：2014-0501-Au-1/4oz
背面图案：北京故宫太和殿、牡丹花
与法国卢浮宫、鸢尾花
设计者：姚有均
浮雕制作者：鲁丹叶　全剑锋　应颖　戴芸

正面图案：中华人民共和国国徽
设计者：中国金币总公司提供
浮雕制作者：集体

编码：2014-0502-Ag-1oz
背面图案：北京天坛祈年殿、中国龙
与法国埃菲尔铁塔、高卢雄鸡
设计者：钟承辛
浮雕制作者：谢欣锐

金币1枚　银币1枚　1 Gold Coin 1 Silver Coin

编码	材质	质量	重量(盎司)	直径(毫米)	面额(元)	成色(%)	最大发行量(枚)	铸造单位
2014-0501-Au-1/4oz	金币	精制	1/4	22	100	99.9	3000	上海
2014-0502-Ag-1oz	银币	精制	1	40	10	99.9	10000	上海

正面图案：中华人民共和国国徽
设计者：中国金币总公司提供
浮雕制作者：集体

编码：2014-0601-Au-1kg
背面图案：万年寺普贤菩萨造像及祥云纹饰
设计者：邓旭
浮雕制作者：张磊

正面图案：中华人民共和国国徽
设计者：中国金币总公司提供
浮雕制作者：集体

编码：2014-0602-Au-5oz
背面图案：四面十方普贤菩萨造像及火焰、祥云纹饰
设计者：王安云
浮雕制作者：常欢　廖博

中国佛教圣地（峨眉山）金银纪念币

Chinese Sacred Buddhist Mountain (Mount Emei) Gold and Silver Commemorative Coins

正面图案：中华人民共和国国徽
设计者：中国金币总公司提供
浮雕制作者：集体

编码：2014-0603-Au-1/4oz
背面图案：报国寺普贤菩萨造像
设计者：王安云
浮雕制作者：宋飞

金币3枚　银币2枚　3 Gold Coins 2 Silver Coins

编码	材质	质量	重量(盎司)	直径(毫米)	面额(元)	成色(%)	最大发行量(枚)	铸造单位
2014-0601-Au-1kg	金币	精制	1公斤	90	10000	99.9	200	深圳
2014-0602-Au-5oz	金币	精制	5	60	2000	99.9	2000	沈阳
2014-0603-Au-1/4oz	金币	精制	1/4	22	100	99.9	40000	深圳
2014-0604-Ag-1kg	银币	精制	1公斤	100	300	99.9	6000	深圳
2014-0605-Ag-2oz	银币	精制	2	40	20	99.9	60000	上海

正面图案：中华人民共和国国徽
设计者：中国金币总公司提供　浮雕制作者：集体

正面图案：中华人民共和国国徽
设计者：中国金币总公司提供
浮雕制作者：集体

编码：2014-0605-Ag-2oz
背面图案：万年寺建筑景观
设计者：邱燕新
浮雕制作者：董慧珍

编码：2014-0604-Ag-1kg
背面图案：金顶景观
设计者：邓旭、魏雪飞　浮雕制作者：李震凯

中国佛教圣地（峨眉山）金银纪念币

Chinese Sacred Buddhist Mountain (Mount Emei) Gold and Silver Commemorative Coins

世界遗产
WORLD HERITAGE · PATRIMOINE MONDIAL

正面图案：中华人民共和国国徽
设计者：中国金币总公司提供　浮雕制作者：集体

编码：2014-0801-Au-1kg
背面图案：飞来峰弥勒佛造像及灵隐寺建筑景观
设计者：常欢　富丽莉　侯继强　浮雕制作者：廖博

世界遗产——杭州西湖文化景观金银纪念币

World Heritage—West Lake Cultural Landscape of Hangzhou Gold and Silver Commemorative Coins

金币3枚　银币5枚　3 Gold Coins 5 Silver Coins

编码	材质	质量	重量(盎司)	直径(毫米)	面额(元)	成色(%)	最大发行量(枚)	铸造单位
2014-0801-Au-1kg	金币	精制	1公斤	90	10000	99.9	200	沈阳
2014-0802-Au-5oz	金币	精制	5	60	2000	99.9	1000	深圳
2014-0803-Au-1/4oz	金币	精制	1/4	22	100	99.9	20000	深圳
2014-0804-Ag-1kg	银币	精制	1公斤	100	300	99.9	3000	上海
2014-0805-Ag-1/2oz	银币	精制	1/2	33	5	99.9	50000	上海
2014-0806-Ag-1/2oz	银币	精制	1/2	33	5	99.9	50000	上海
2014-0807-Ag-1/2oz	银币	精制	1/2	33	5	99.9	50000	上海
2014-0808-Ag-1/2oz	银币	精制	1/2	33	5	99.9	50000	沈阳

共同正面
正面图案：中华人民共和国国徽
设计者：中国金币总公司提供
浮雕制作者：集体

编码：2014-0802-Au-5oz
背面图案："三潭印月"及苏堤、雷峰塔等景观
设计者：姚有均
浮雕制作者：邓姗姗

编码：2014-0803-Au-1/4oz
背面图案："西泠印社"景观
设计者：陈莉
浮雕制作者：姜茜茜　钟承辛

共同正面
正面图案：中华人民共和国国徽
设计者：中国金币总公司提供　浮雕制作者：集体

编码：2014-0805-Ag-1/2oz
背面图案："苏堤春晓"景观
设计者：白荣国　宋飞　浮雕制作者：朱熙华　鲁丹叶　全剑锋

编码：2014-0806-Ag-1/2oz
背面图案："曲院风荷"景观
设计者：李果　浮雕制作者：陈彦文　戴芸　应颖

编码：2014-0807-Ag-1/2oz
背面图案："平湖秋月"景观
设计者：李果　浮雕制作者：朱熙华　鲁丹叶　全剑锋

编码：2014-0808-Ag-1/2oz
背面图案："断桥残雪"景观
设计者：白荣国　浮雕制作者：韩晓生　常欢

正面图案：中华人民共和国国徽
设计者：中国金币总公司提供　浮雕制作者：集体

世界遗产——杭州西湖文化景观金银纪念币

World Heritage – West Lake Cultural Landscape of Hangzhou Gold and Silver Commemorative Coins

编码：2014-0804-Ag-1kg
背面图案：西湖全景图
设计者：王云野　王刚　安乐　周卓　浮雕制作者：王文栋　黄喆

新疆生产建设兵团成立60周年金银纪念币

The 60th Anniversary of Xinjiang Production and Construction Corps Gold and Silver Commemorative Coins

正面图案：中华人民共和国国徽
设计者：中国金币总公司提供
浮雕制作者：集体

编码：2014-0901-Au-1/4oz
背面图案：兵团战士坚苦创业、屯垦戍边场景
设计者：朱熙华
浮雕制作者：宋飞

编码：2014-0903-Ag-1oz
背面图案：兵团建设绿色生态屏障
设计者：朱熙华
浮雕制作者：张春晔

共同正面
正面图案：中华人民共和国国徽
设计者：中国金币总公司提供
浮雕制作者：集体

编码：2014-0902-Ag-5oz
背面图案：兵团60年建设辉煌成就
设计者：朱熙华
浮雕制作者：邓姗姗　钟永辛　李震凯

金币1枚　银币2枚　1 Gold Coin　2 Silver Coins

编码	材质	质量	重量(盎司)	直径(毫米)	面额(元)	成色(%)	最大发行量(枚)	铸造单位
2014-0901-Au-1/4oz	金币	精制	1/4	22	100	99.9	10000	深圳
2014-0902-Ag-5oz	银币	精制	5	70	50	99.9	3000	深圳
2014-0903-Ag-1oz	银币	精制	1	40	10	99.9	20000	上海

新疆生产建设兵团成立60周年金银纪念币

The 60th Anniversary of Xinjiang Production and Construction Corps Gold and Silver Commemorative Coins

共同正面
正面图案：中华人民共和国国徽
设计者：中国金币总公司提供　浮雕制作者：集体

编码：2014-1102-Au-1/4oz
背面图案：商代人面龙纹盉
设计者：朱熙华　浮雕制作者：邓姗姗　刘雨浓

编码：2014-1101-Au-5oz
背面图案：商代后母戊方鼎
设计者：朱熙华　浮雕制作者：徐云飞

中国青铜器金银纪念币（第3组）

The Chinese Bronze Ware Gold and Silver Commemorative Coins(3rd Issue)

金币2枚　银币3枚　2 Gold Coins 3 Silver Coins

编码	材质	质量	重量(盎司)	直径(毫米)	面额(元)	成色(%)	最大发行量(枚)	铸造单位
2014-1101-Au-5oz	金币	精制	5	60	2000	99.9	1000	上海
2014-1102-Au-1/4oz	金币	精制	1/4	22	100	99.9	30000	深圳
2014-1103-Ag-1kg	银币	精制	1公斤	100	300	99.9	4000	上海
2014-1104-Ag-5oz	银币	精制	5	70	50	99.9	6000	深圳
2014-1105-Ag-1oz	银币	精制	1	40	10	99.9	60000	深圳

正面图案：中华人民共和国国徽
设计者：中国金币总公司提供
浮雕制作者：集体

编码：2014-1103-Ag-1kg
背面图案：商代亚址方尊
设计者：朱熙华
浮雕制作者：陈彦文

中国青铜器金银纪念币（第3组）

The Chinese Bronze Ware Gold and Silver Commemorative Coins(3rd Issue)

正面图案：中华人民共和国国徽
设计者：中国金币总公司提供
浮雕制作者：集体

编码：2014-1104-Ag-5oz
背面图案：商代亚醜方罍
设计者：朱熙华
浮雕制作者：钟承辛

正面图案：中华人民共和国国徽
设计者：中国金币总公司提供
浮雕制作者：集体

编码：2014-1105-Ag-1oz
背面图案：商代龙纹觥
设计者：朱熙华
浮雕制作者：贵庆东

2014北京国际钱币博览会银质纪念币

The Commemorative Silver Coin for Beijing International Coin Exposition 2014

正面图案：象征钱币、地球的点线图案与2014北京国际钱币博览会会标
设计者：朱熙华
浮雕制作者：禹飞

编码：2014-1201-Ag-1oz
背面图案：中国清代乾隆通宝钱币与西班牙双柱钱币
设计者：齐云兰
浮雕制作者：田晓斌

银币1枚　1 Silver Coin

编码	材质	质量	重量(盎司)	直径(毫米)	面额(元)	成色(%)	最大发行量(枚)	铸造单位
2014-1201-Ag-1oz	银币	精制	1	40	10	99.9	30000	深圳

2014北京国际钱币博览会银质纪念币

The Commemorative Silver Coin for Beijing International Coin Exposition 2014

图书在版编目（CIP）数据

中华人民共和国贵金属纪念币图录. 2010-2014 / 武亚越，冯建主编. 一成都：西南财经大学出版社，2015.12

ISBN 978-7-5504-2167-7

I. ①中… II. ①武… ②冯… III. ①纪念币—中国—图录 IV. ①F822.2-64②J526.6

中国版本图书馆CIP数据核字（2015）第221213号

书　　名：**中华人民共和国贵金属纪念币图录 2010-2014**
名誉主编：徐联初　张汉桥
主　　编：武亚越　冯　建

总 监 制：冯　建
责任编辑：穆志坚
助理编辑：傅倩宇
装帧设计：白少二
责任印制：封俊川
电脑制作：阿　林

出版发行：西南财经大学出版社（四川省成都市光华村街55号）
制　　版：成都跨克创意文化传播有限公司
印　　刷：雅昌文化（集团）有限公司
版　　次：2015年12月第1版
印　　次：2015年12月第1次印刷
成品尺寸：280mm×280mm
印　　张：18
插　　页：10
字　　数：230千字
印　　数：1-2000册
定　　价：480.00元
书　　号：ISBN 978-7-5504-2167-7